Madame Cat

Nancy Peña

Let's rock, everybody, let's rock!
Everybody in the whole cell block
Was dancing to the jailhouse rock!

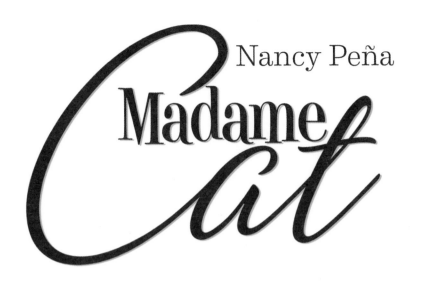

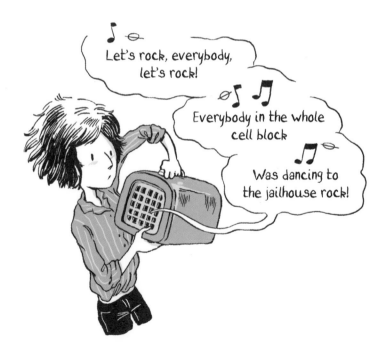

Life Drawn

NANCY PEÑA
Story & Art

*

MARK BENCE
Translation

PIERRE BISSON
Lettering

*

FABRICE SAPOLSKY
& ALEX DONOGHUE
U.S. Edition Editors

VINCENT HENRY
Original Edition Editor

JERRY FRISSEN
Senior Art Director

FABRICE GIGER
Publisher

Rights & Licensing - licensing@humanoids.com
Press and Social Media - pr@humanoids.com

MADAME CAT
This title is a publication of Humanoids, Inc. 8033 Sunset Blvd. #628, Los Angeles, CA 90046.
Copyright © 2018 Humanoids, Inc., Los Angeles (USA). All rights reserved.
Humanoids and its logos are ® and © 2018 Humanoids, Inc.

Life Drawn is an imprint of Humanoids, Inc.

First published in France under the title "Madame" — Copyright © 2015-2016 La Boîte à Bulles & Nancy Peña.
All rights reserved. All characters, the distinctive likenesses thereof and all related indicia are trademarks
of La Boîte à Bulles Sarl and / or of Nancy Peña.

Madame arrives

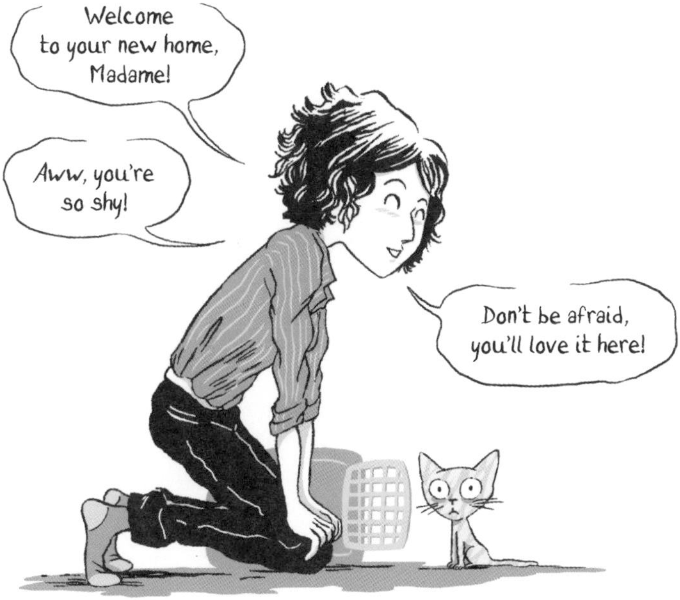
Welcome to your new home, Madame!
Aww, you're so shy!
Don't be afraid, you'll love it here!

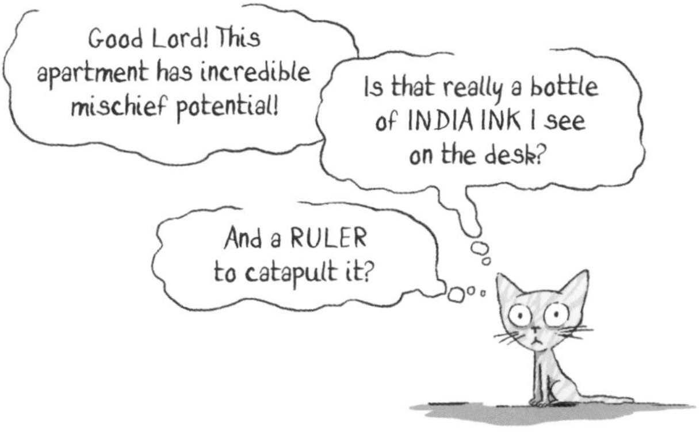
Good Lord! This apartment has incredible mischief potential!
Is that really a bottle of INDIA INK I see on the desk?
And a RULER to catapult it?

Madame emerges

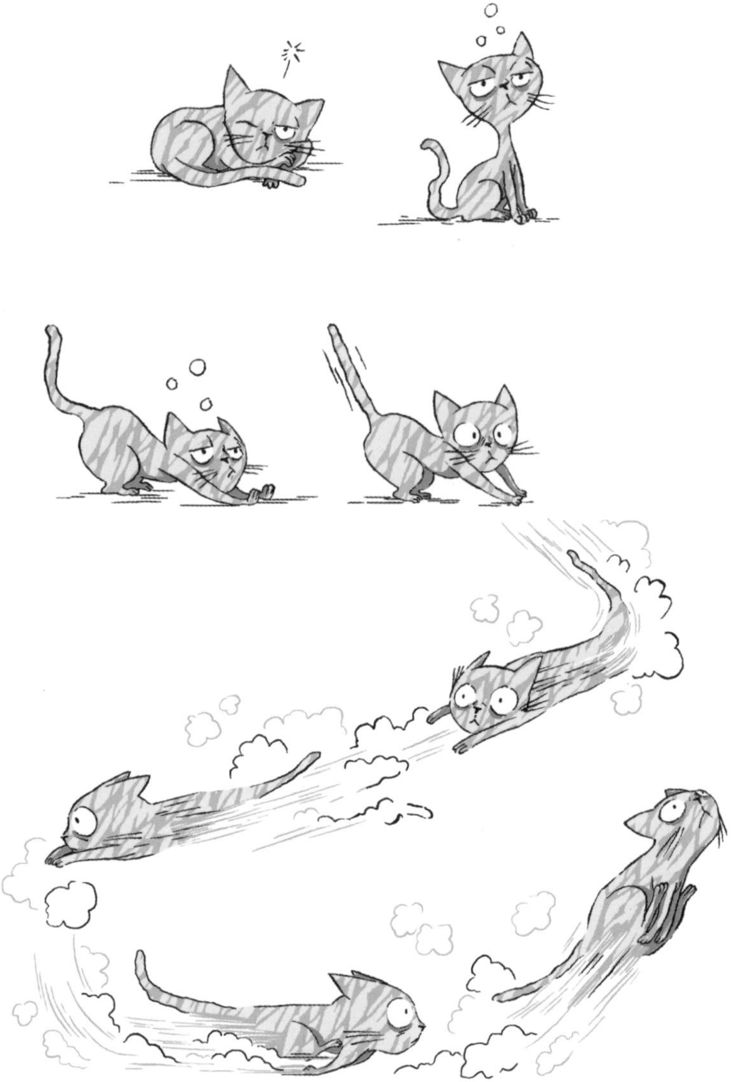

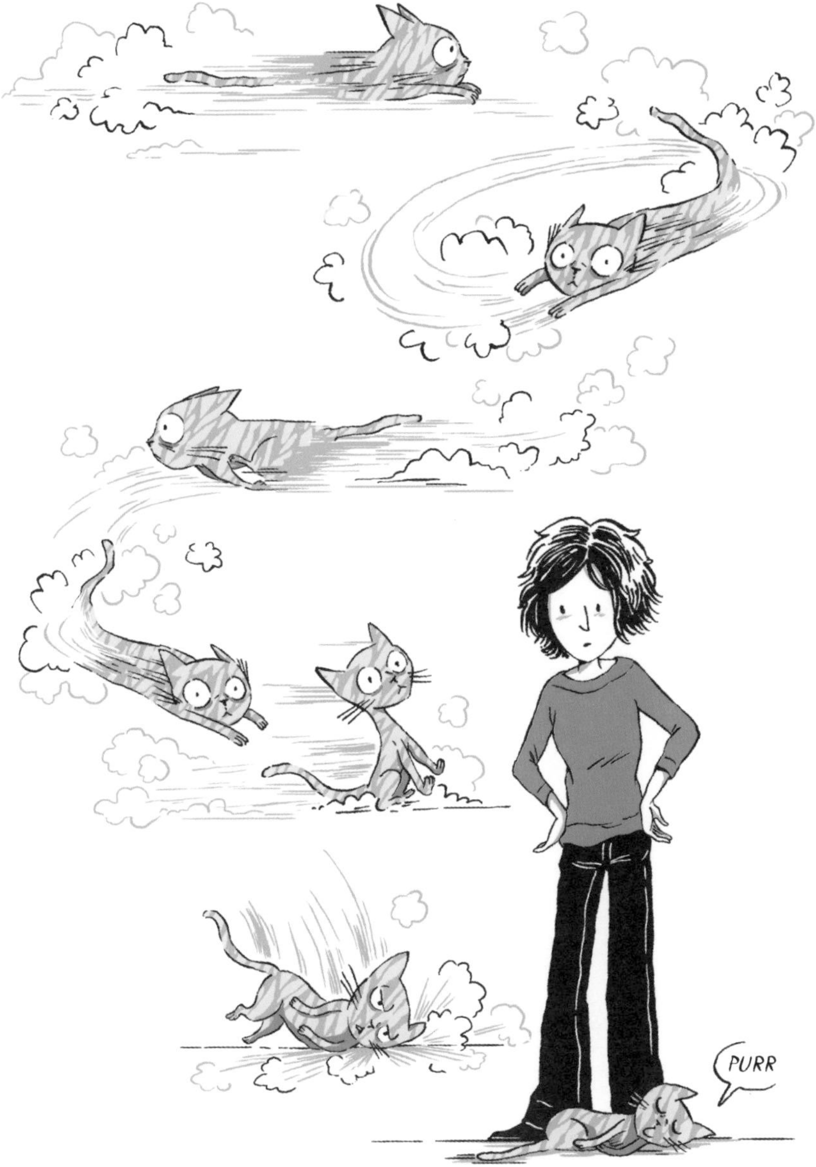
PURR

Madame plunges

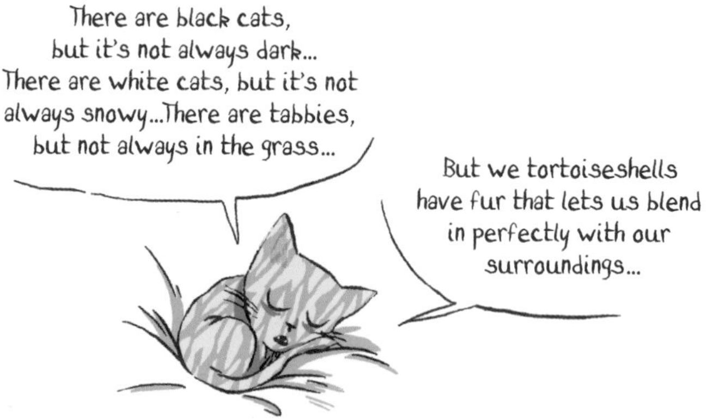
There are black cats, but it's not always dark... There are white cats, but it's not always snowy...There are tabbies, but not always in the grass...
But we tortoiseshells have fur that lets us blend in perfectly with our surroundings...

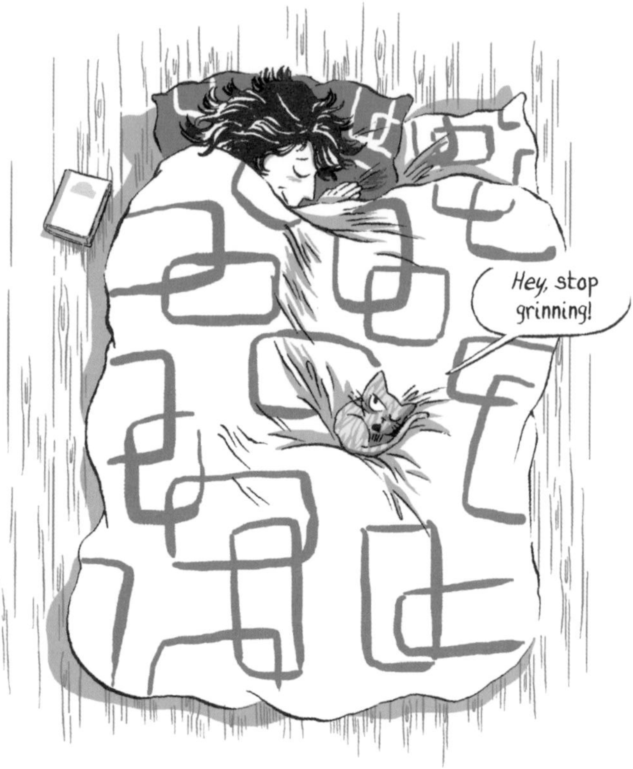
Hey, stop grinning!

Madame settles in

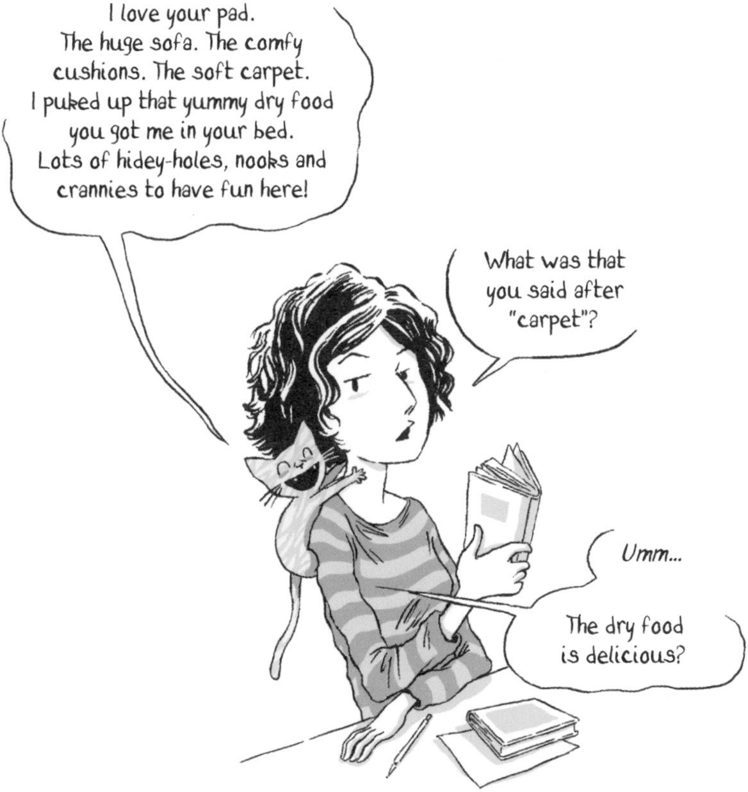
I love your pad.
The huge sofa. The comfy cushions. The soft carpet. I puked up that yummy dry food you got me in your bed. Lots of hidey-holes, nooks and crannies to have fun here!
What was that you said after "carpet"?
Umm...
The dry food is delicious?

Madame exorcizes

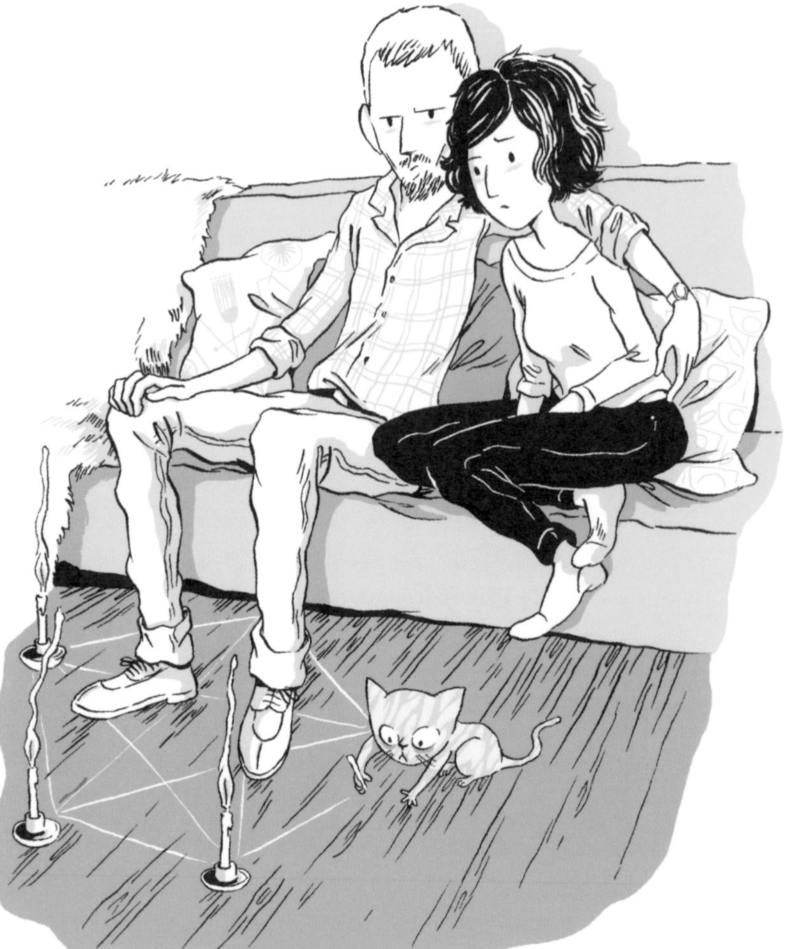

Madame in limbo

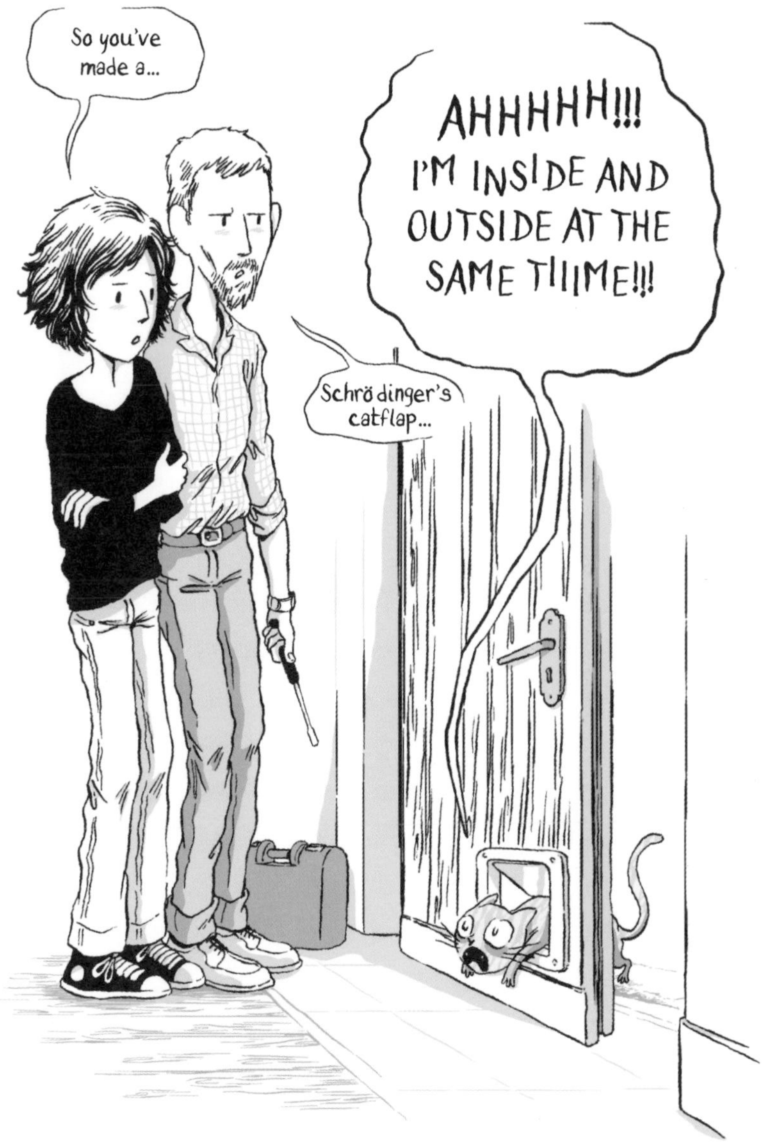
So you've made a...
Schrödinger's catflap...
AHHHHH!!! I'M INSIDE AND OUTSIDE AT THE SAME TIIIME!!!

Madame flirts

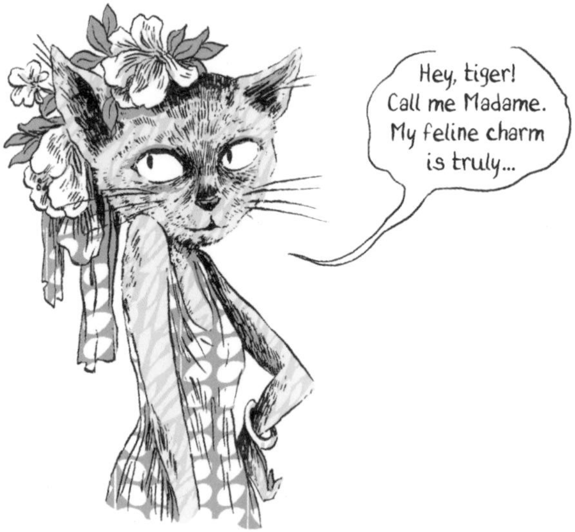
Hey, tiger! Call me Madame. My feline charm is truly...

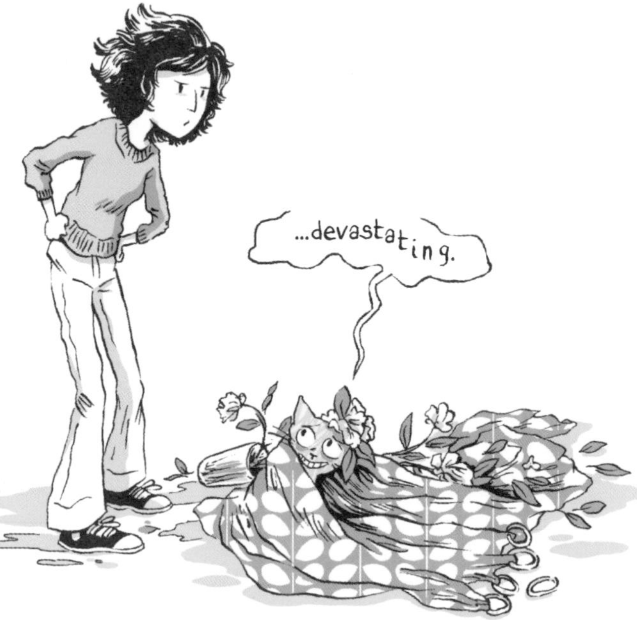
...devastating.

Madame suggests

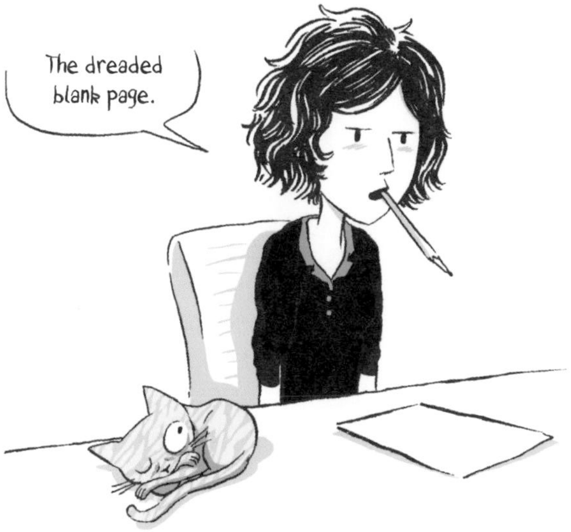
The dreaded blank page.

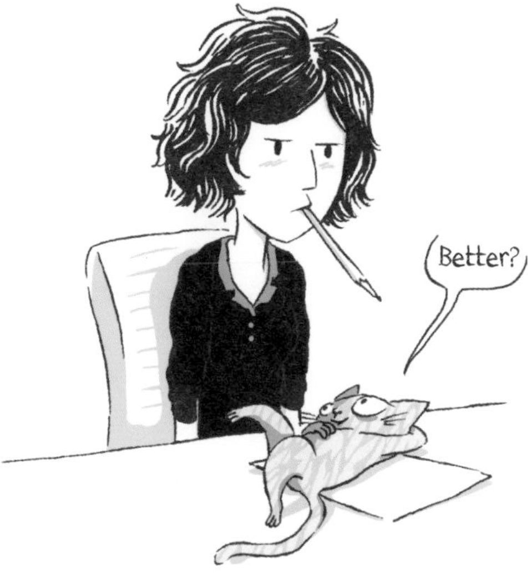
Better?

Madame untangles

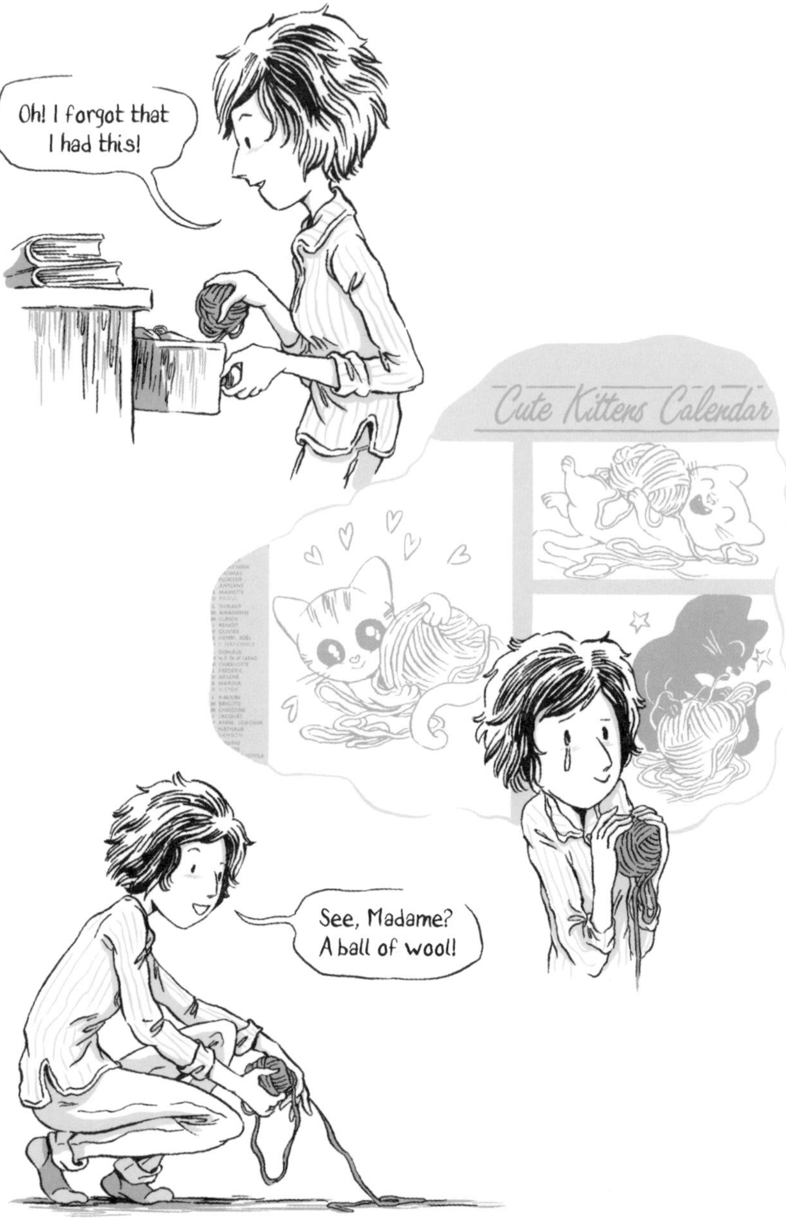
Oh! I forgot that I had this!
Cute Kittens Calendar
See, Madame? A ball of wool!

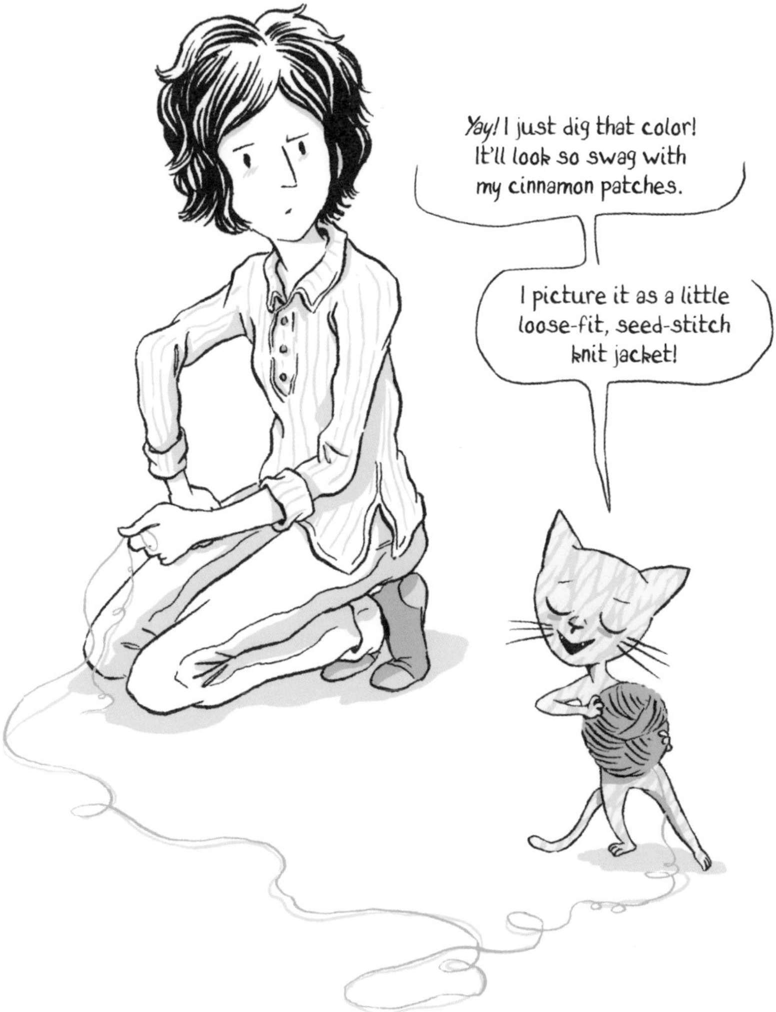
Yay! I just dig that color! It'll look so swag with my cinnamon patches.
I picture it as a little loose-fit, seed-stitch knit jacket!

Madame splatters

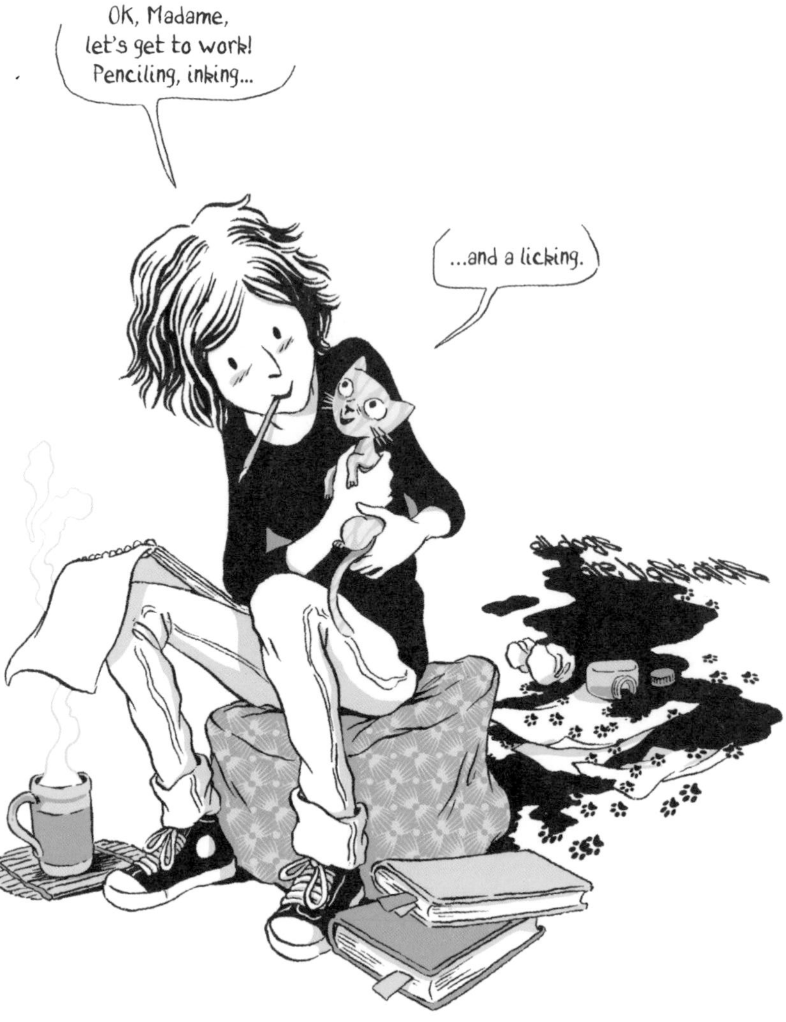

OK, Madame, let's get to work! Penciling, inking...
...and a licking.

Madame gives in

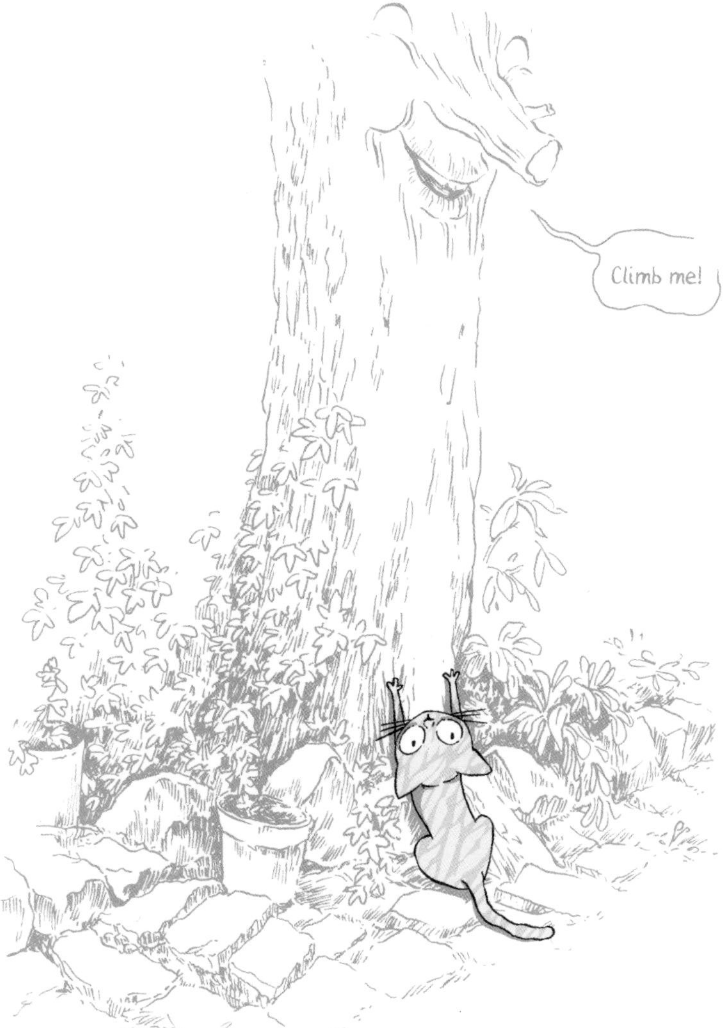
Climb me!

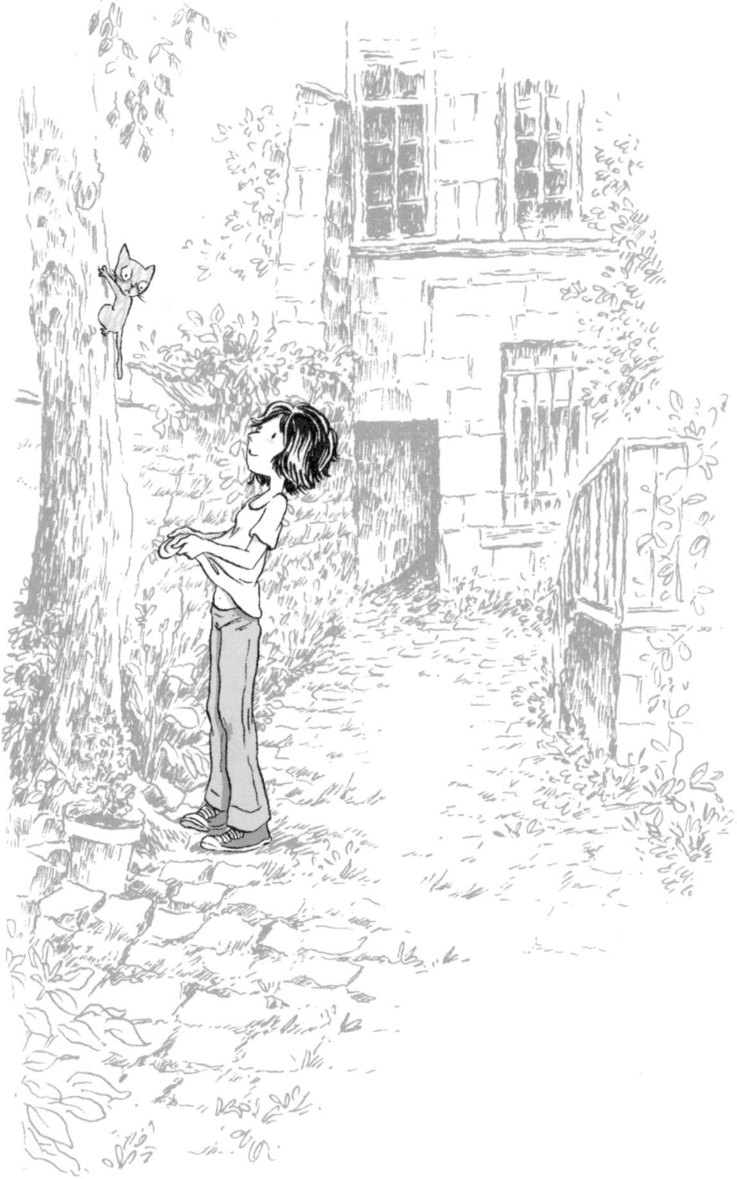

Madame cringes

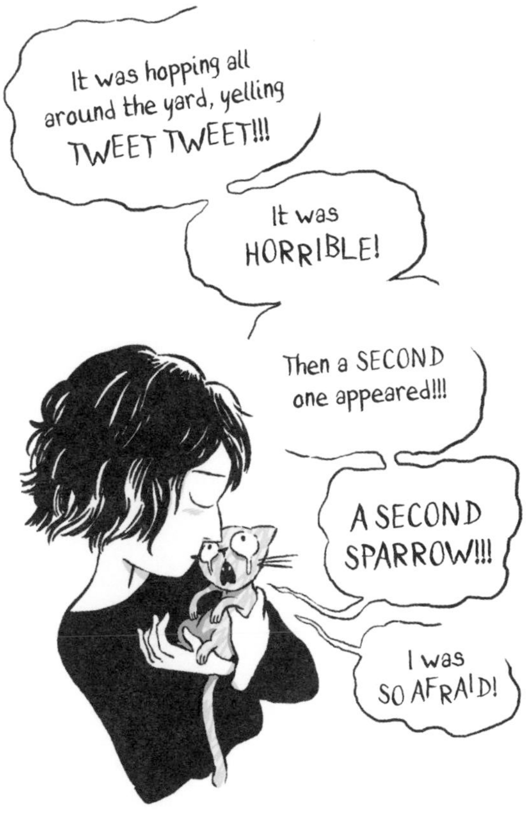

It was hopping all around the yard, yelling TWEET TWEET!!!
It was HORRIBLE!
Then a SECOND one appeared!!!
A SECOND SPARROW!!!
I was SO AFRAID!

Madame questions

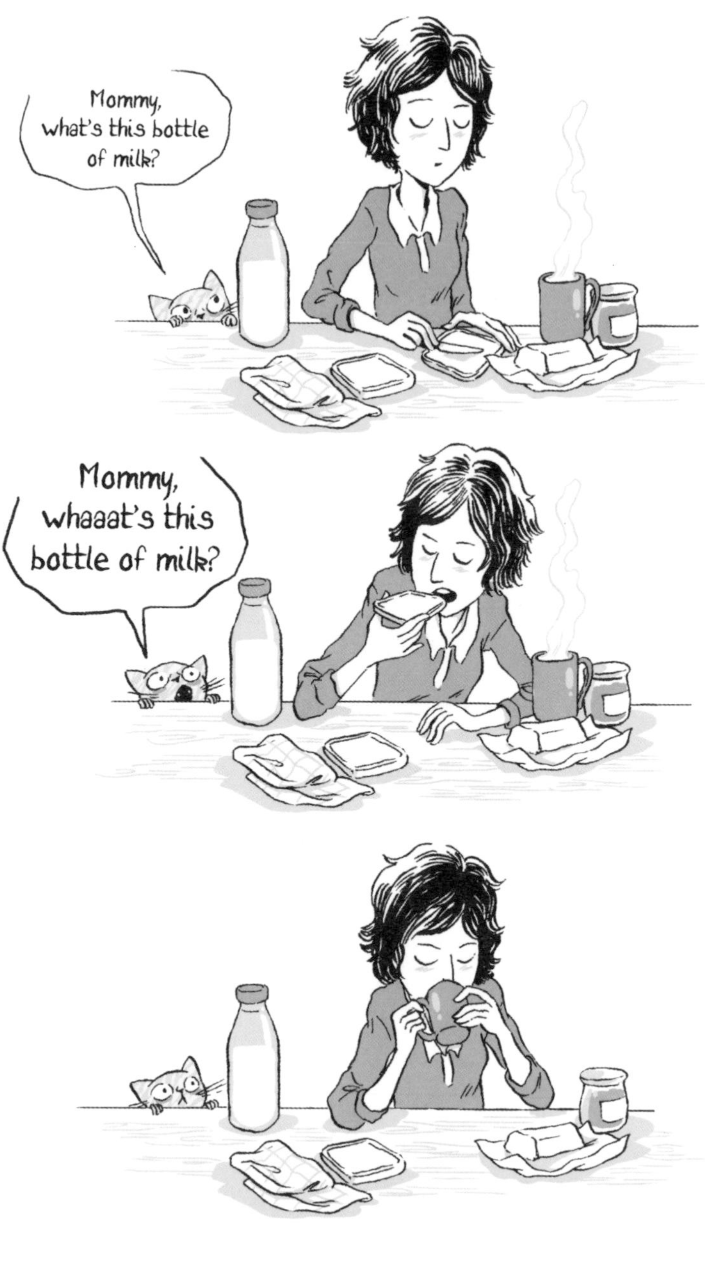
Mommy, what's this bottle of milk?
Mommy, whaaat's this bottle of milk?

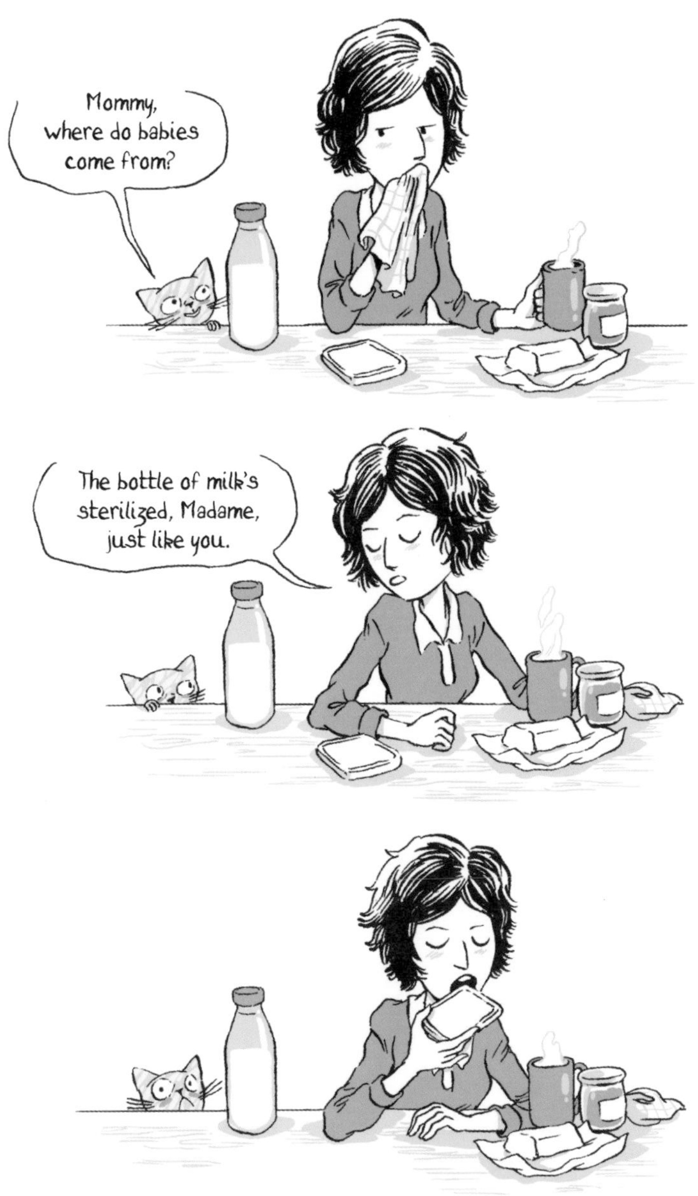
Mommy, where do babies come from?
The bottle of milk's sterilized, Madame, just like you.

Madame designs

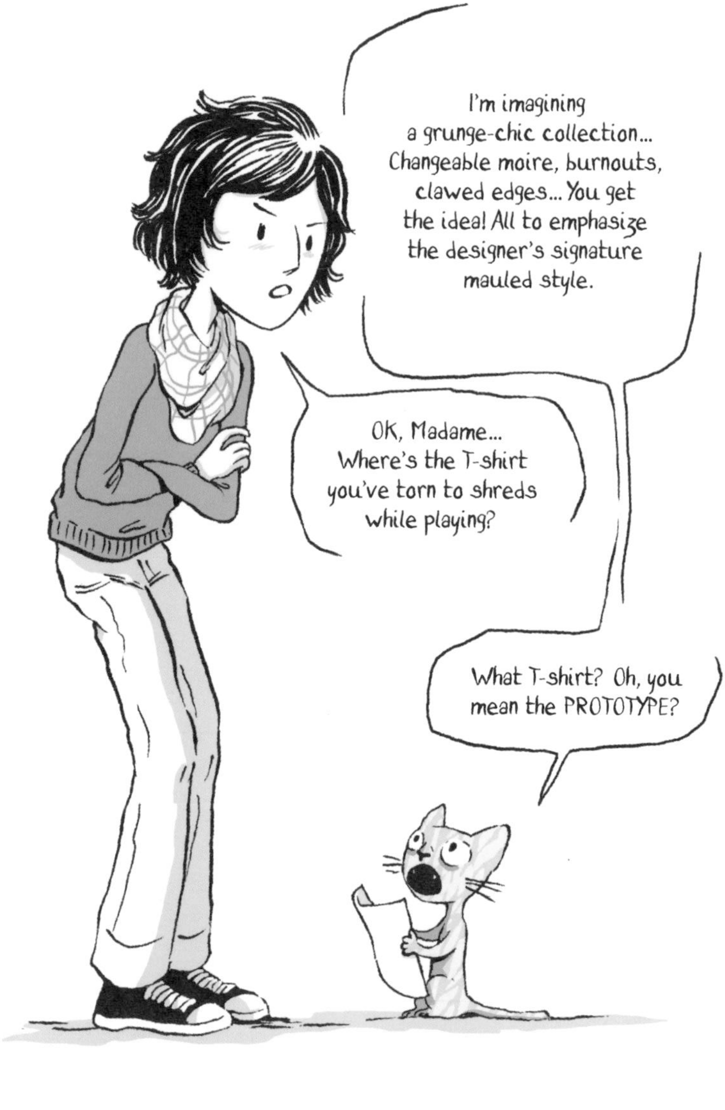
I'm imagining a grunge-chic collection... Changeable moire, burnouts, clawed edges... You get the idea! All to emphasize the designer's signature mauled style.
OK, Madame... Where's the T-shirt you've torn to shreds while playing?
What T-shirt? Oh, you mean the PROTOTYPE?

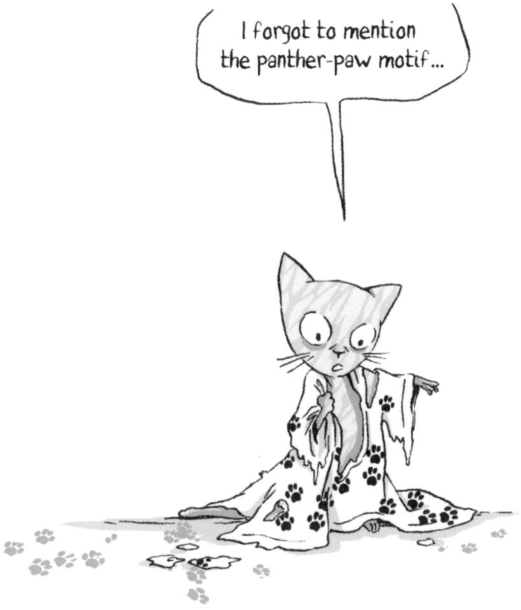
I forgot to mention the panther-paw motif...

Madame freezes

Madame stalks

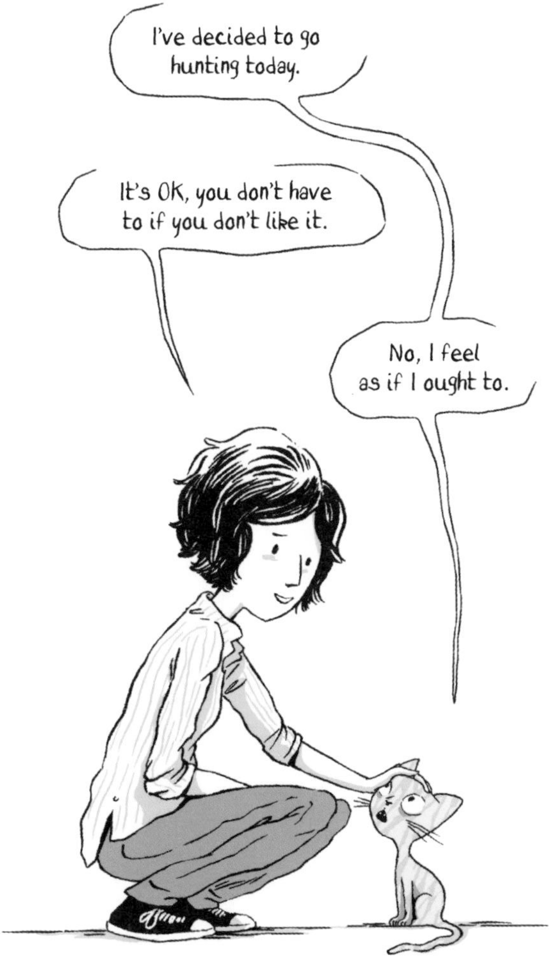
I've decided to go hunting today.
It's OK, you don't have to if you don't like it.
No, I feel as if I ought to.

Madame concedes

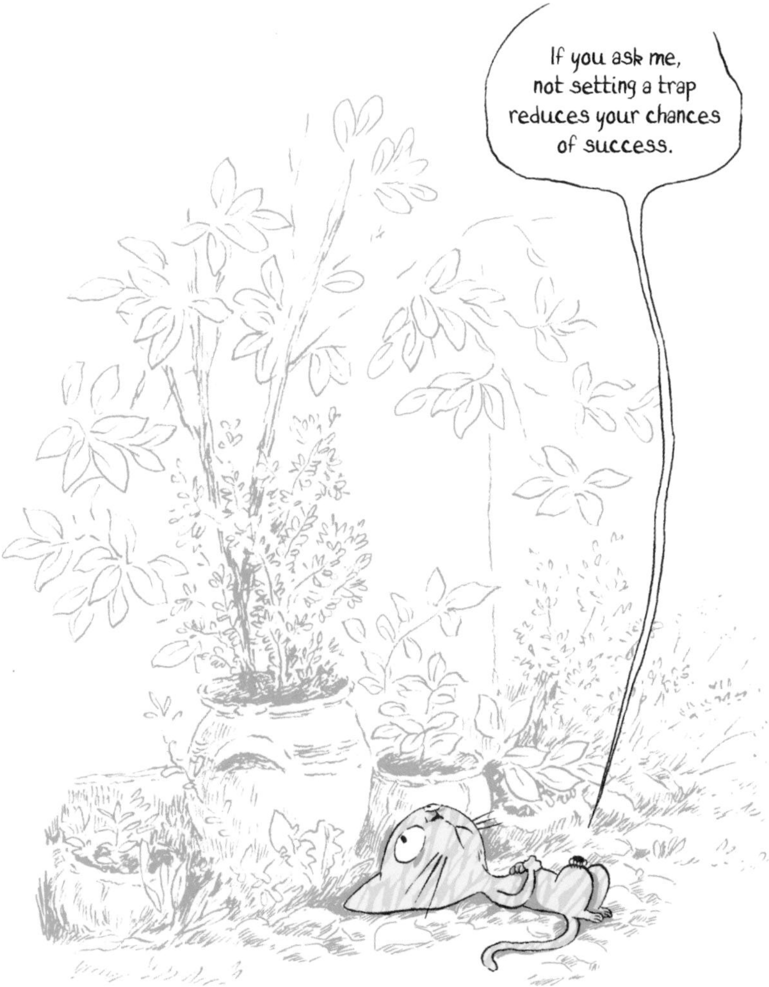

If you ask me, not setting a trap reduces your chances of success.

Madame inherits

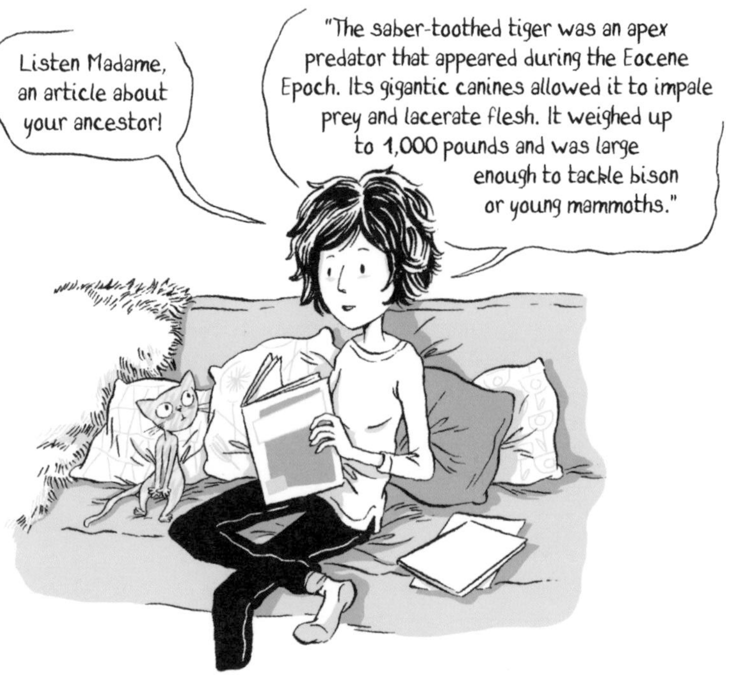
Listen Madame, an article about your ancestor!
"The saber-toothed tiger was an apex predator that appeared during the Eocene Epoch. Its gigantic canines allowed it to impale prey and lacerate flesh. It weighed up to 1,000 pounds and was large enough to tackle bison or young mammoths."

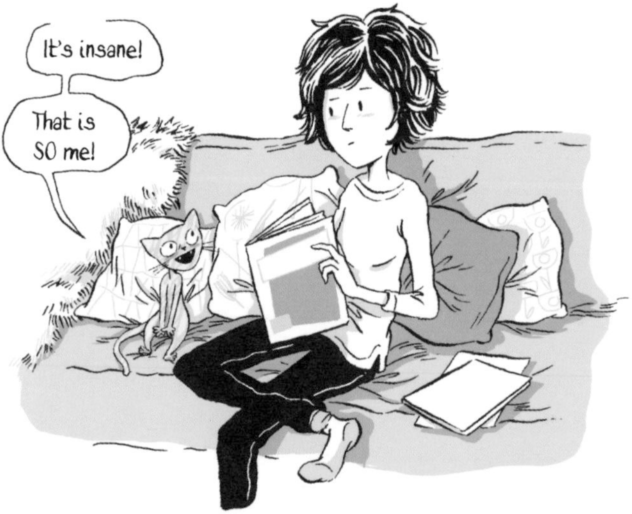
It's insane!
That is SO me!

Madame insists

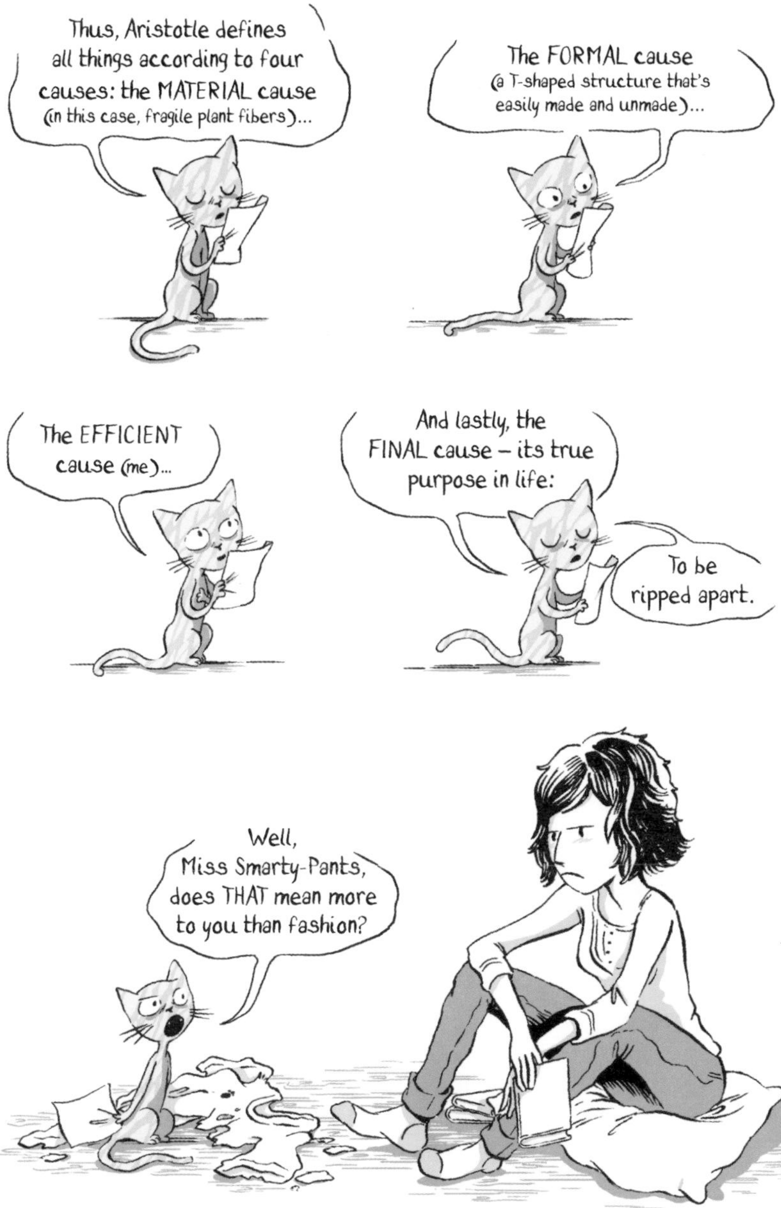
Thus, Aristotle defines all things according to four causes: the MATERIAL cause (in this case, fragile plant fibers)...
The FORMAL cause (a T-shaped structure that's easily made and unmade)...
The EFFICIENT cause (me)...
And lastly, the FINAL cause – its true purpose in life:
To be ripped apart.
Well, Miss Smarty-Pants, does THAT mean more to you than fashion?

Madame smells

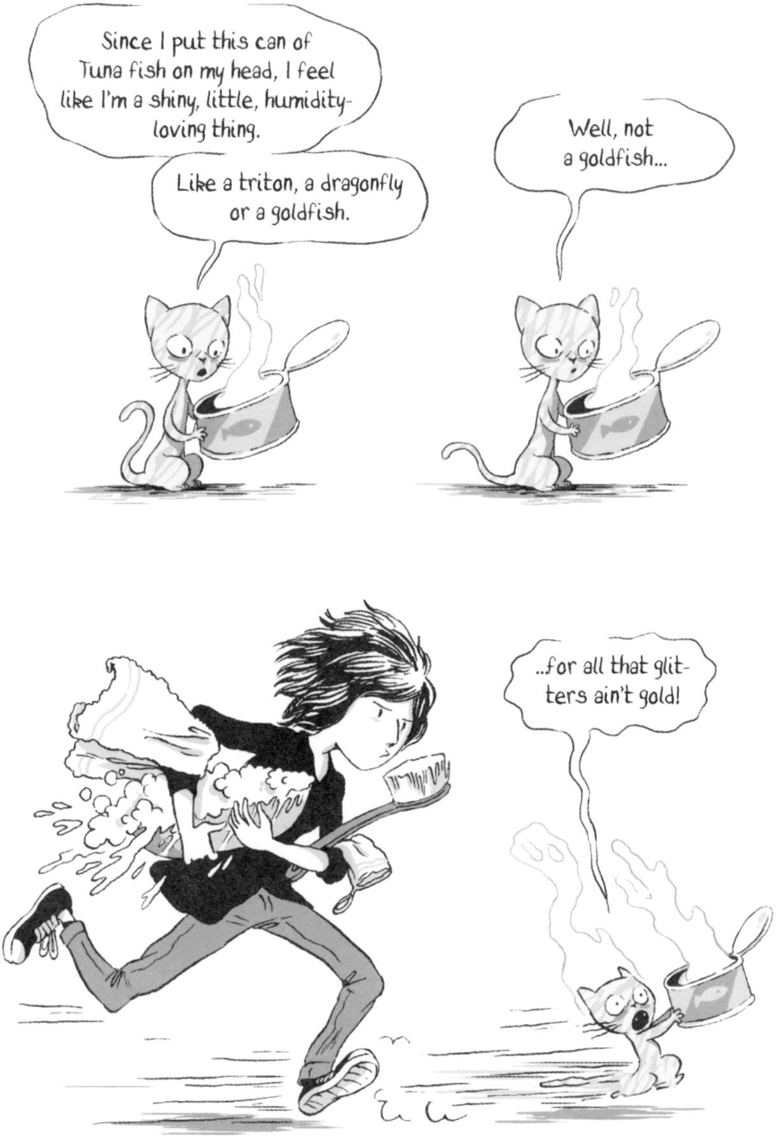
Since I put this can of Tuna fish on my head, I feel like I'm a shiny, little, humidity-loving thing.
Like a triton, a dragonfly or a goldfish.
Well, not a goldfish...
...for all that glit-ters ain't gold!

Madame flounders

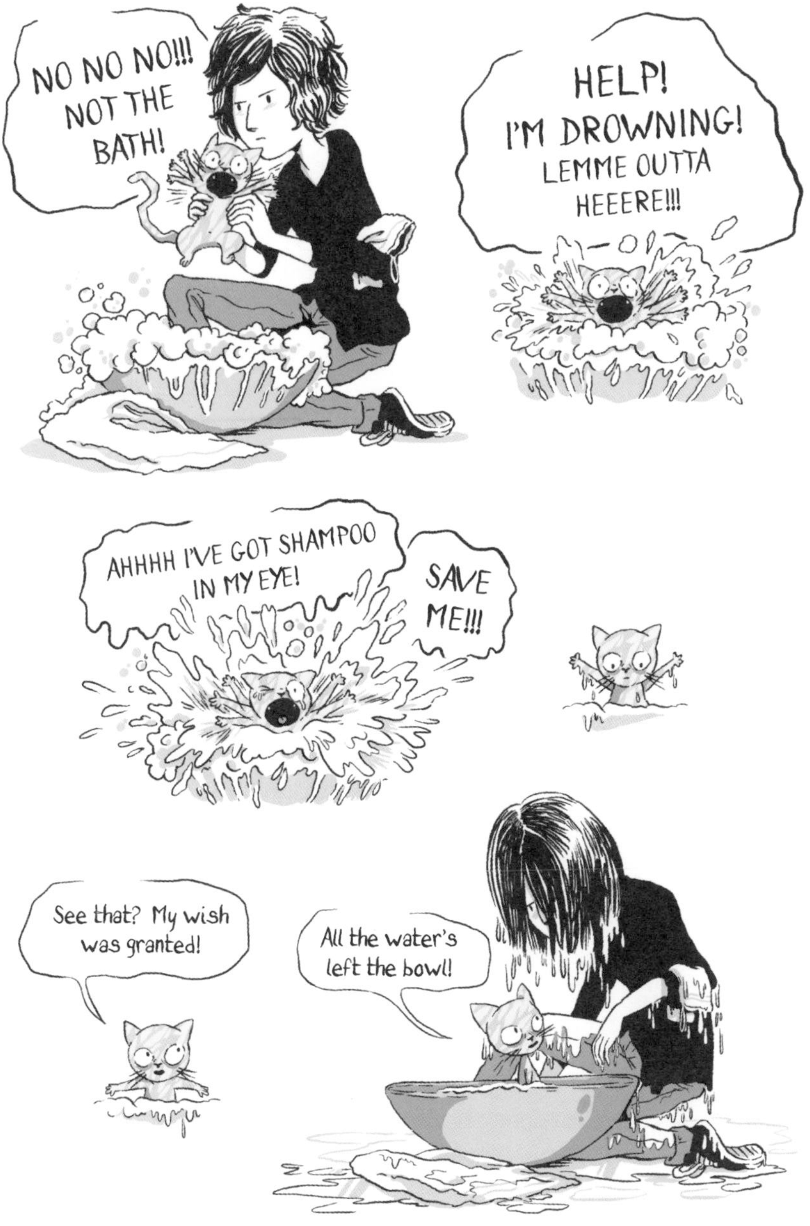
NO NO NO!!! NOT THE BATH!
HELP! I'M DROWNING! LEMME OUTTA HEEERE!!!
AHHHH I'VE GOT SHAMPOO IN MY EYE!
SAVE ME!!!
See that? My wish was granted!
All the water's left the bowl!

Madame ZIPs

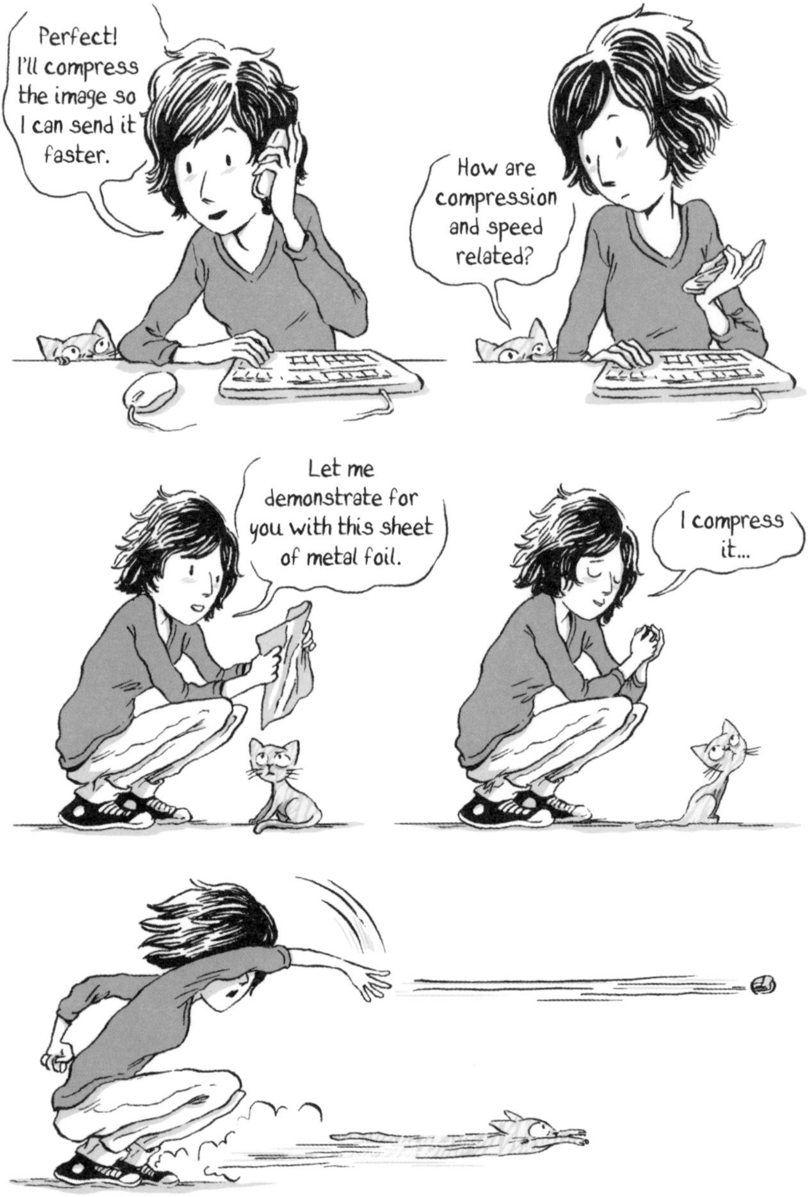
Perfect! I'll compress the image so I can send it faster.
How are compression and speed related?
Let me demonstrate for you with this sheet of metal foil.
I compress it...

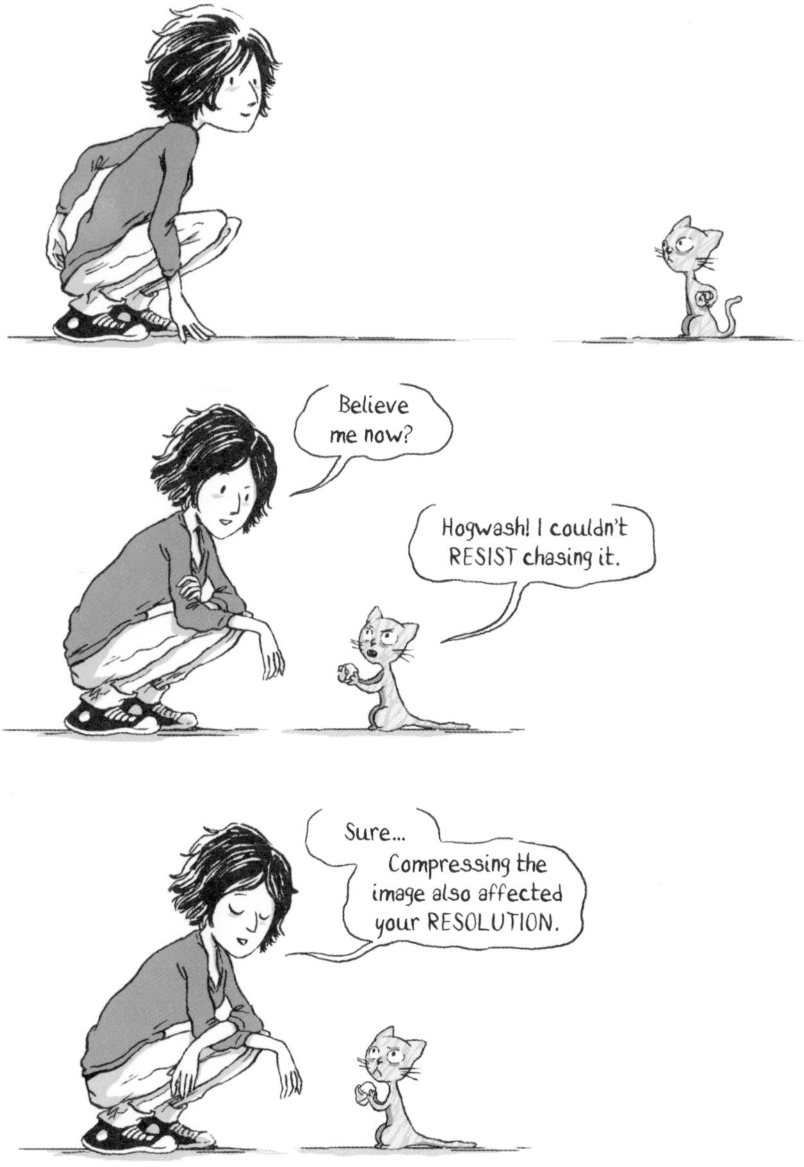
Believe me now?
Hogwash! I couldn't RESIST chasing it.
Sure... Compressing the image also affected your RESOLUTION.

Madame bones up

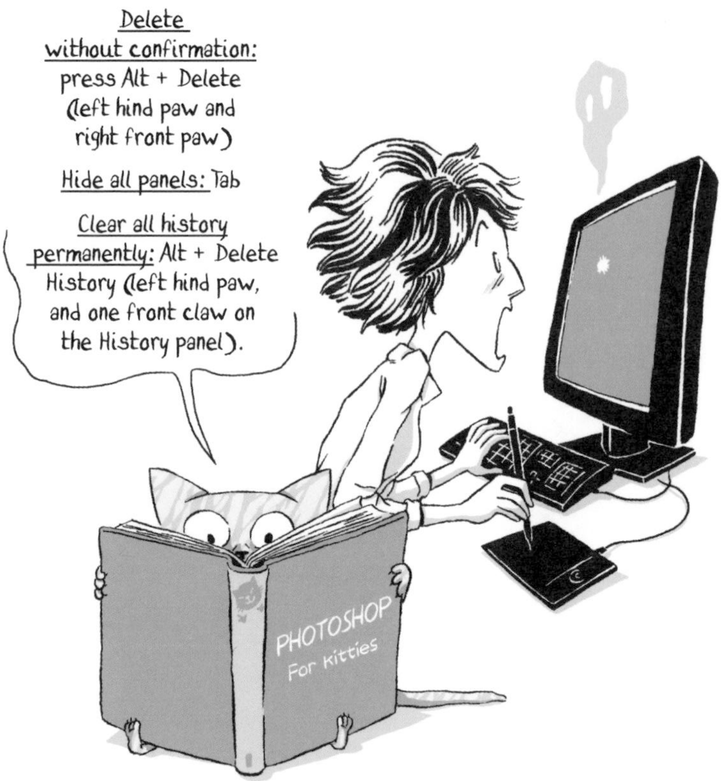
Delete without confirmation: press Alt + Delete (left hind paw and right front paw)
Hide all panels: Tab
Clear all history permanently: Alt + Delete History (left hind paw, and one front claw on the History panel).
PHOTOSHOP For kitties

Madame clashes

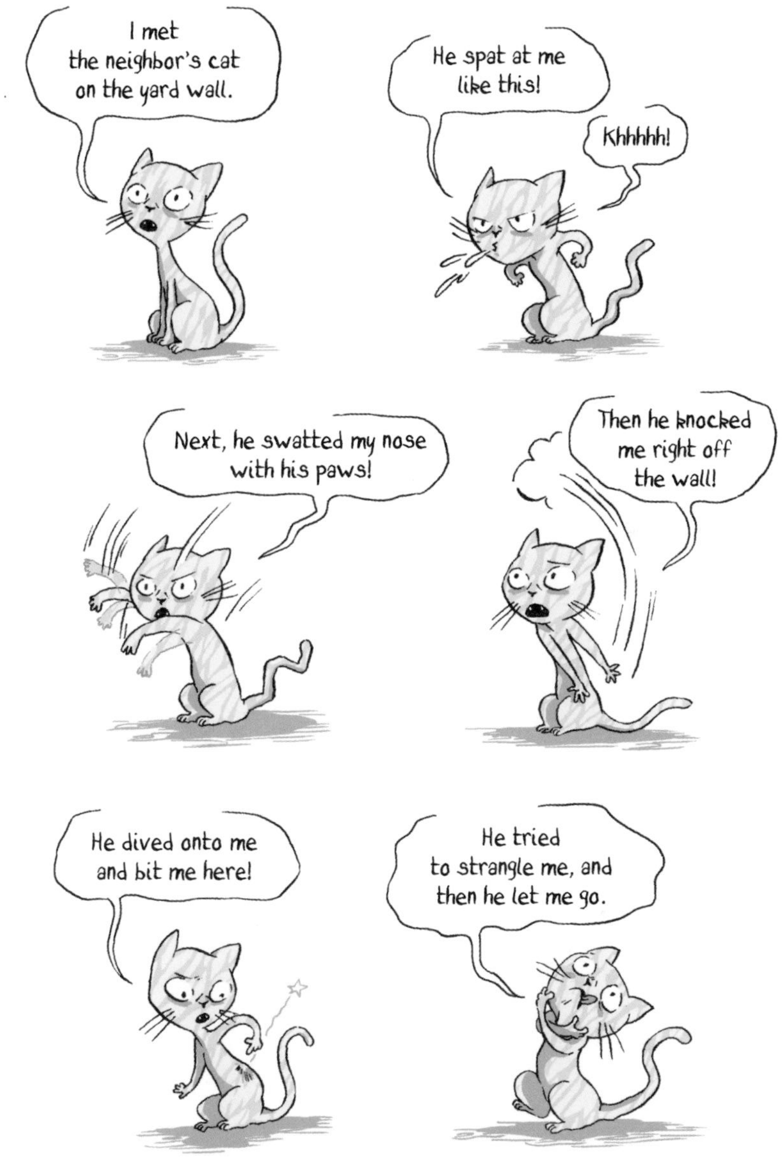
I met the neighbor's cat on the yard wall.
He spat at me like this!
Khhhhh!
Next, he swatted my nose with his paws!
Then he knocked me right off the wall!
He dived onto me and bit me here!
He tried to strangle me, and then he let me go.

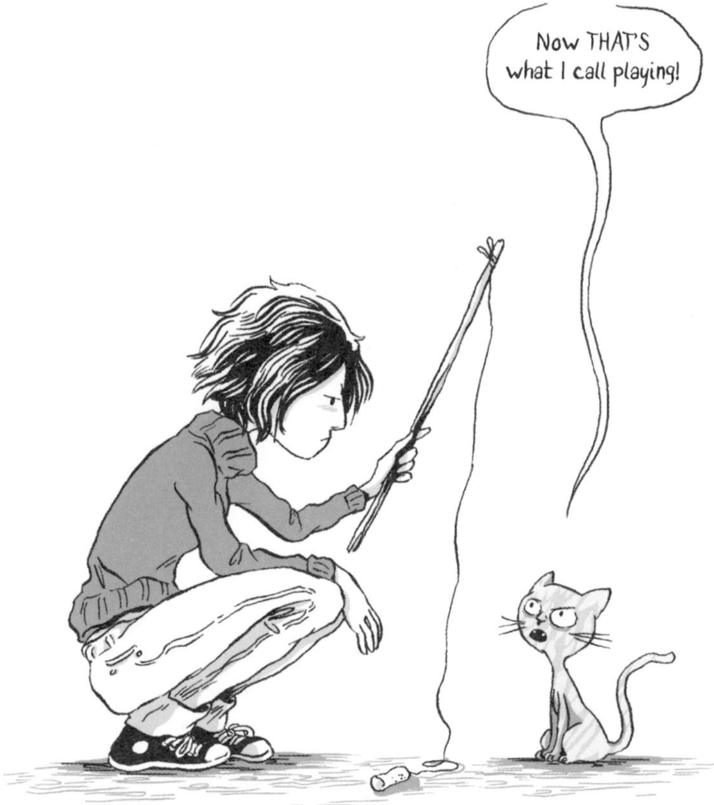
Now THAT'S what I call playing!

Madame persists

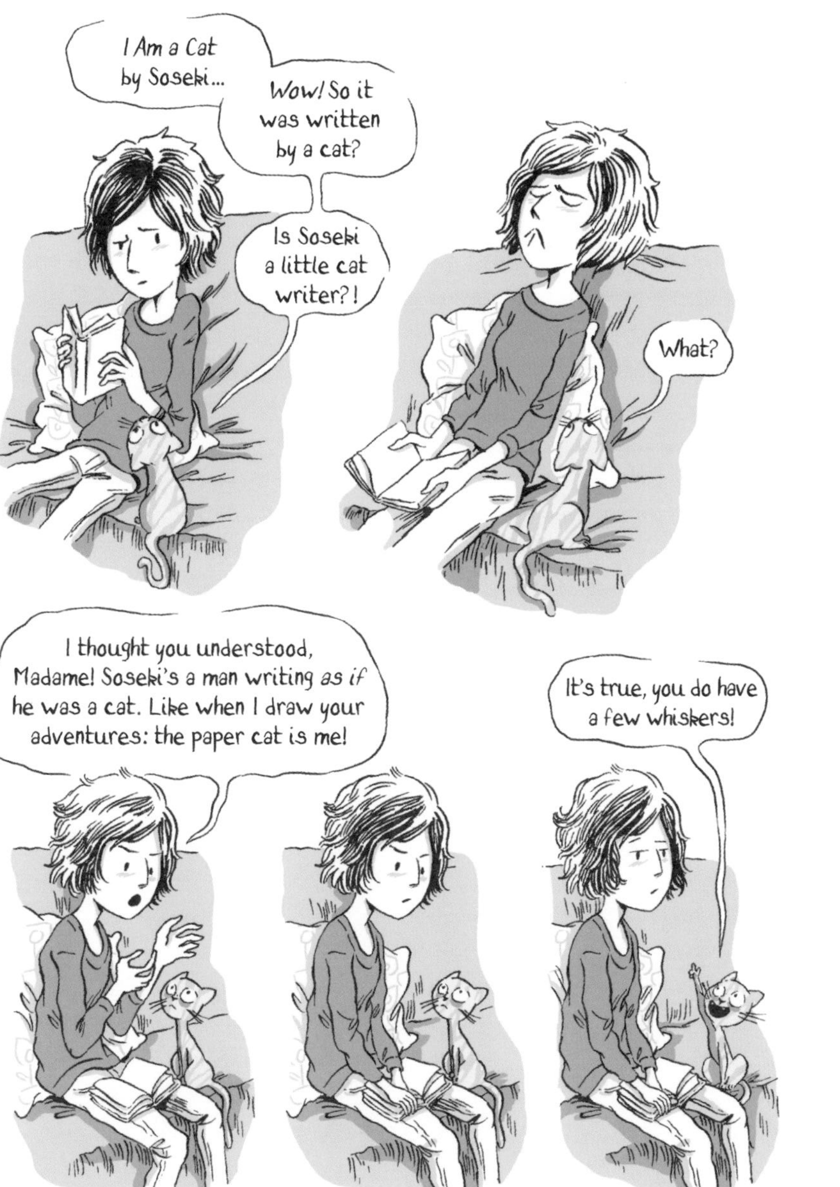
I Am a Cat by Soseki...
Wow! So it was written by a cat?
Is Soseki a little cat writer?!
What?
I thought you understood, Madame! Soseki's a man writing *as if* he was a cat. Like when I draw your adventures: the paper cat is me!
It's true, you do have a few whiskers!

Madame connives

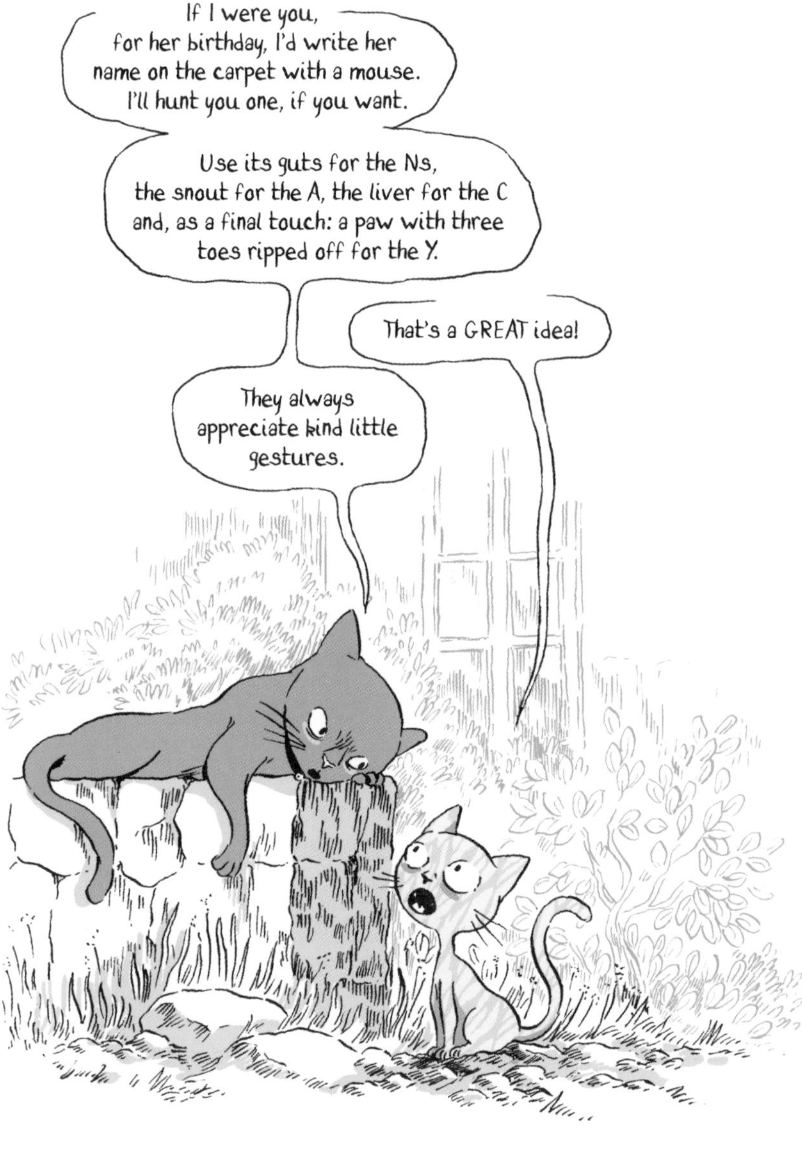
If I were you, for her birthday, I'd write her name on the carpet with a mouse. I'll hunt you one, if you want.
Use its guts for the Ns, the snout for the A, the liver for the C and, as a final touch: a paw with three toes ripped off for the Y.
They always appreciate kind little gestures.
That's a GREAT idea!

Oh, my GOD, Madame!
That's it, she's found it!

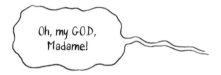

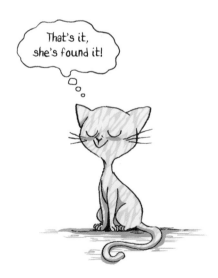

Madame optimizes

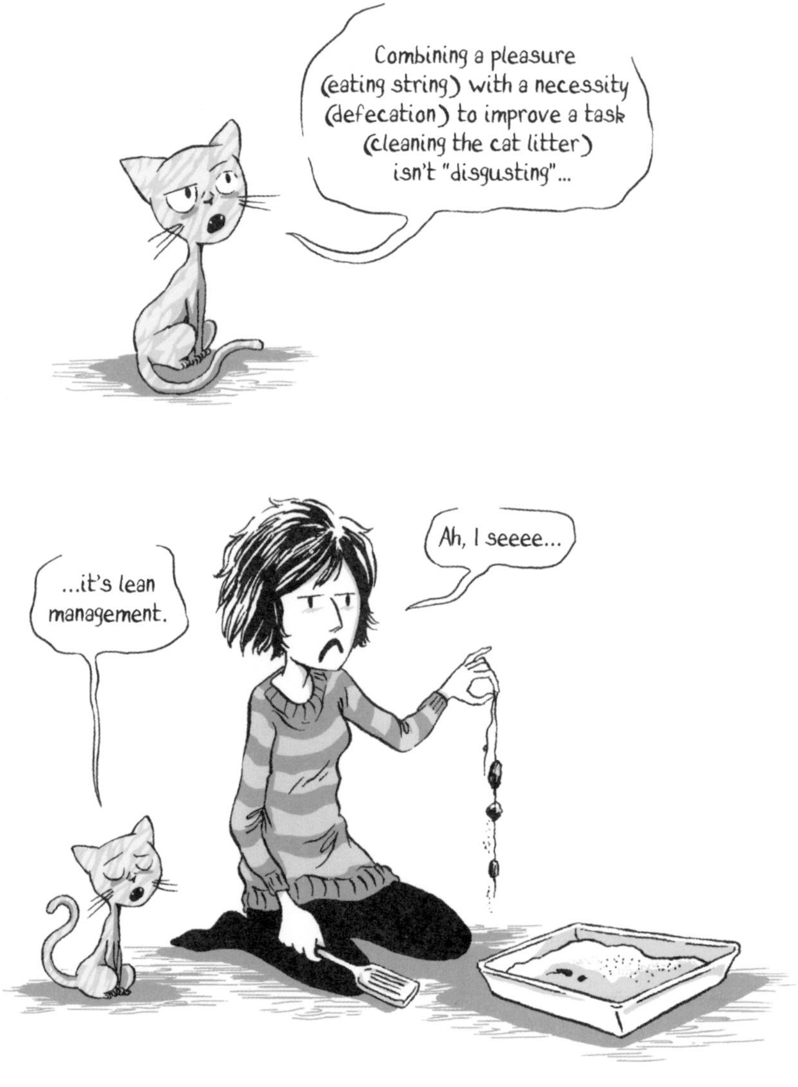
Combining a pleasure (eating string) with a necessity (defecation) to improve a task (cleaning the cat litter) isn't "disgusting"...
Ah, I seeee...
...it's lean management.

Madame digests

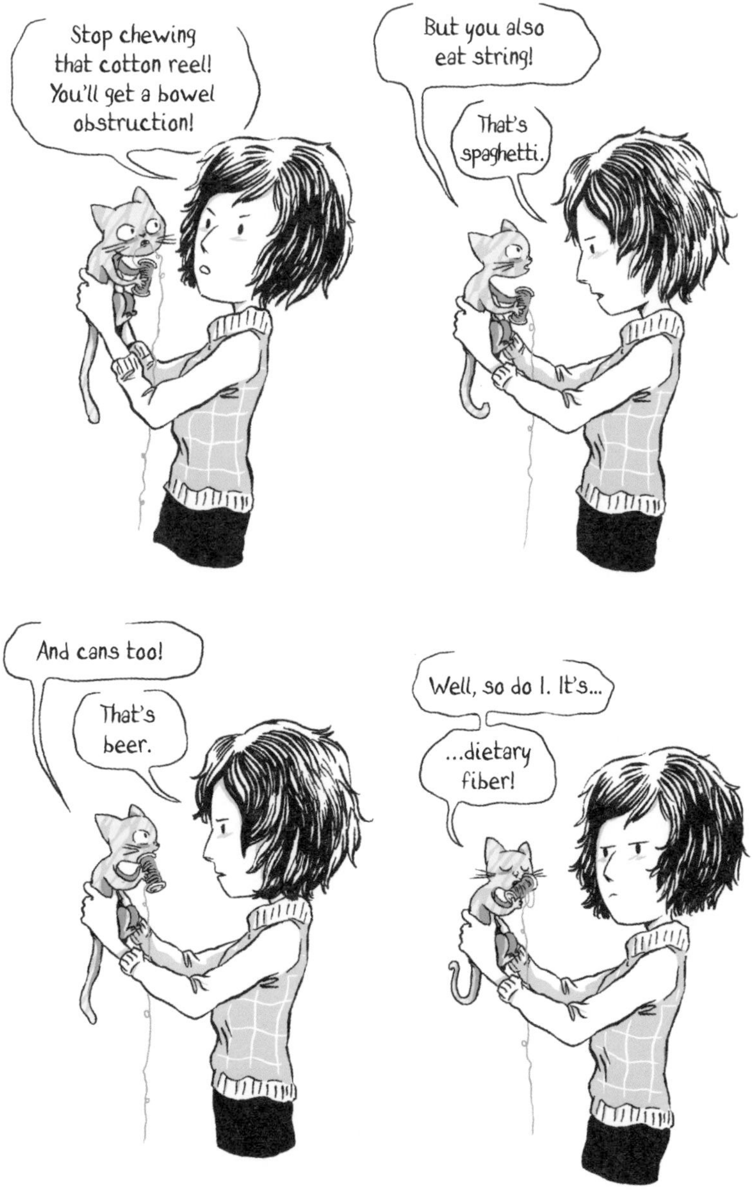
Stop chewing that cotton reel! You'll get a bowel obstruction!
But you also eat string!
That's spaghetti.
And cans too!
That's beer.
Well, so do I. It's...
...dietary fiber!

Madame mediates

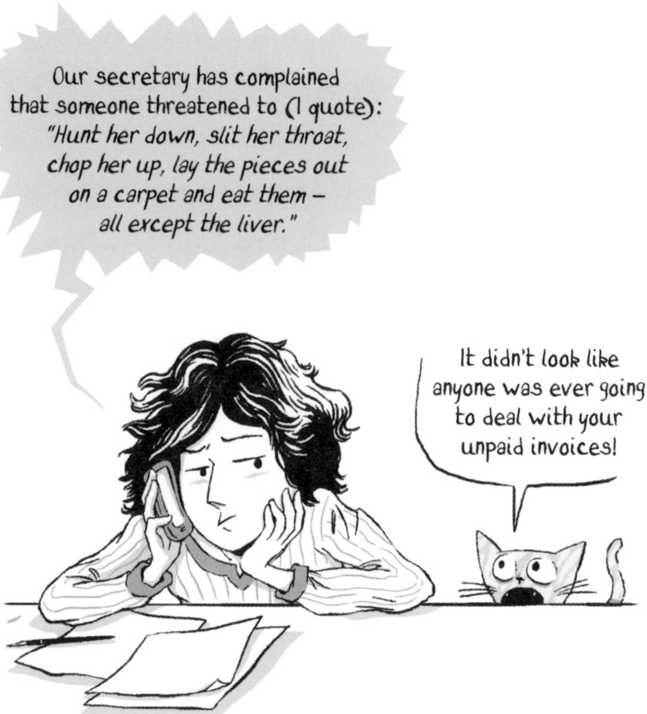
Our secretary has complained that someone threatened to (I quote): *"Hunt her down, slit her throat, chop her up, lay the pieces out on a carpet and eat them – all except the liver."*
It didn't look like anyone was ever going to deal with your unpaid invoices!

Madame reanimates

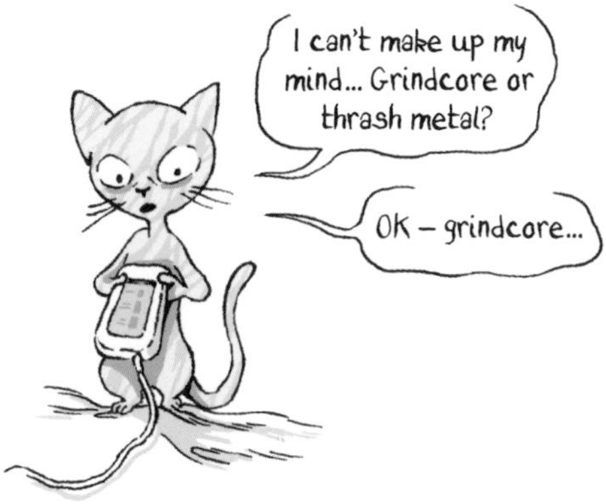
I can't make up my mind... Grindcore or thrash metal?
OK – grindcore...

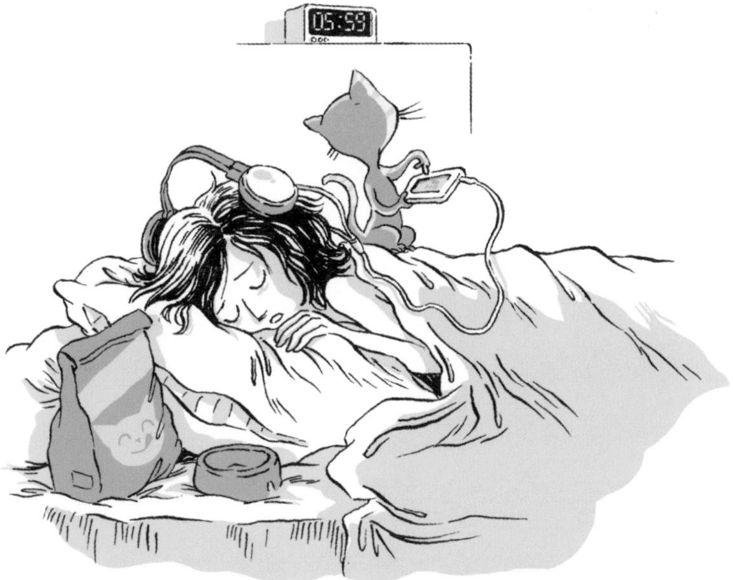
05:59

Madame views

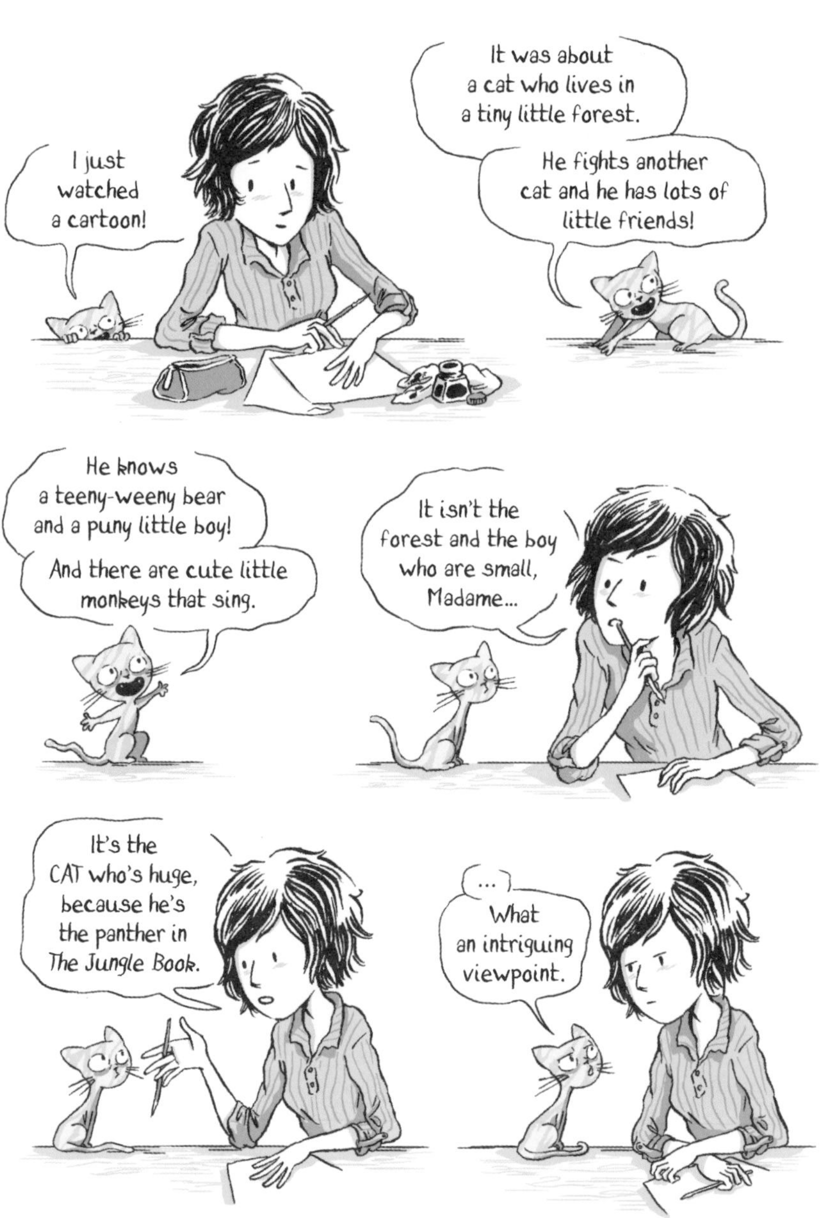
I just watched a cartoon!
It was about a cat who lives in a tiny little forest.
He fights another cat and he has lots of little friends!
He knows a teeny-weeny bear and a puny little boy!
And there are cute little monkeys that sing.
It isn't the forest and the boy who are small, Madame...
It's the CAT who's huge, because he's the panther in The Jungle Book.
...
What an intriguing viewpoint.

Madame laments

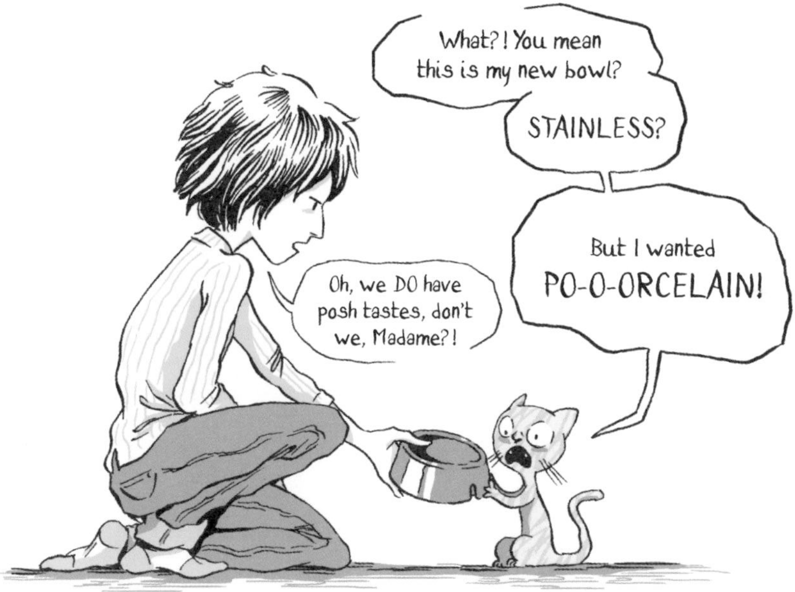
What?! You mean this is my new bowl?
STAINLESS?
But I wanted PO-O-ORCELAIN!
Oh, we DO have posh tastes, don't we, Madame?!

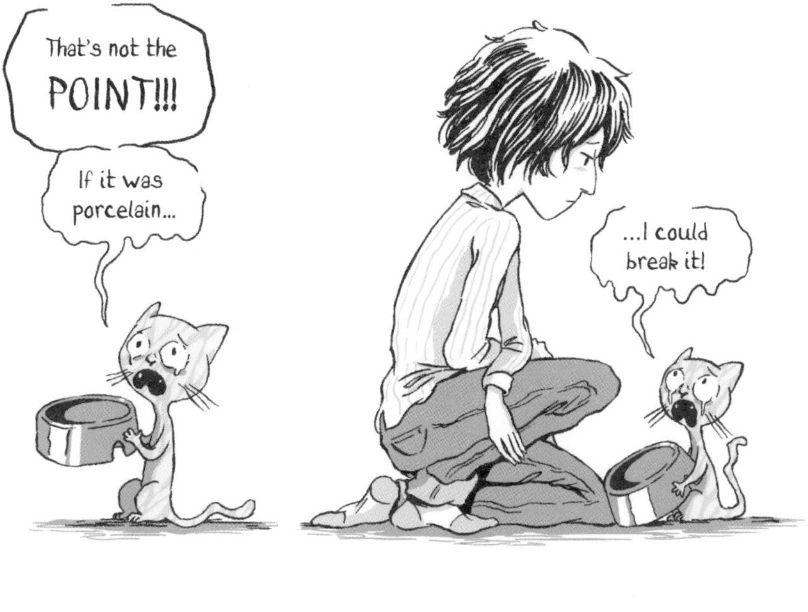
That's not the POINT!!!
If it was porcelain...
...I could break it!

Madame sips

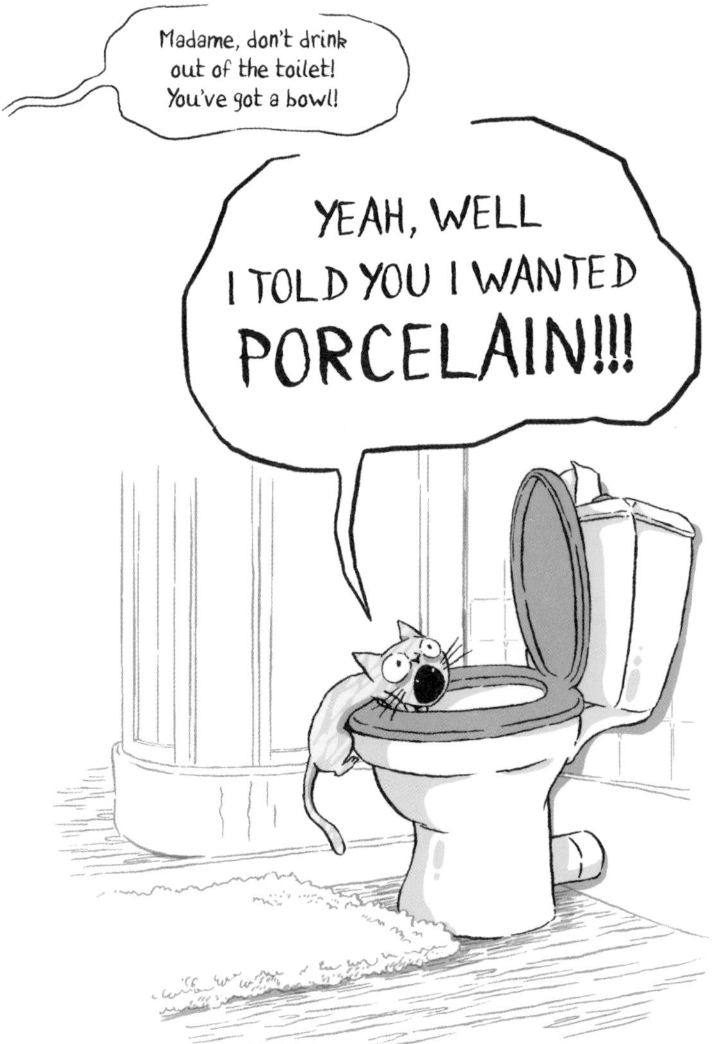
Madame, don't drink out of the toilet! You've got a bowl!
YEAH, WELL I TOLD YOU I WANTED PORCELAIN!!!

Madame alarms

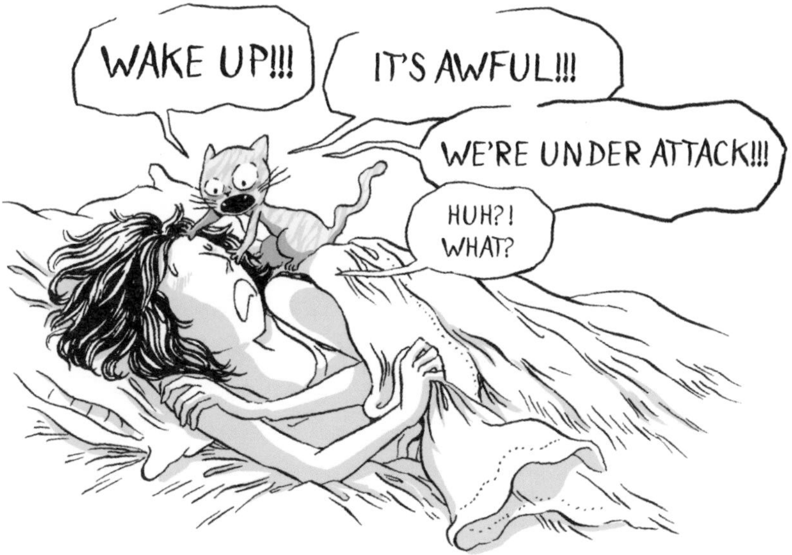
WAKE UP!!!
IT'S AWFUL!!!
WE'RE UNDER ATTACK!!!
HUH?! WHAT?

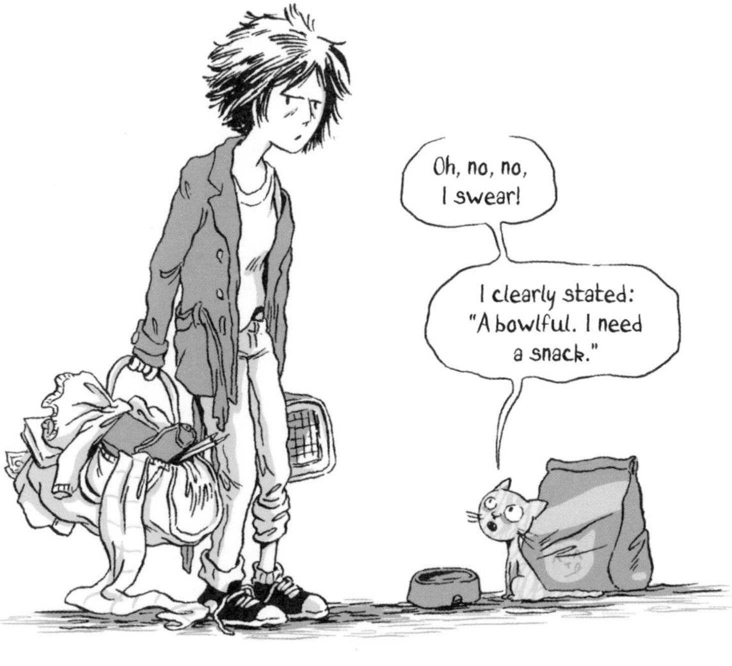
Oh, no, no, I swear!
I clearly stated: "A bowlful. I need a snack."

Madame pounces

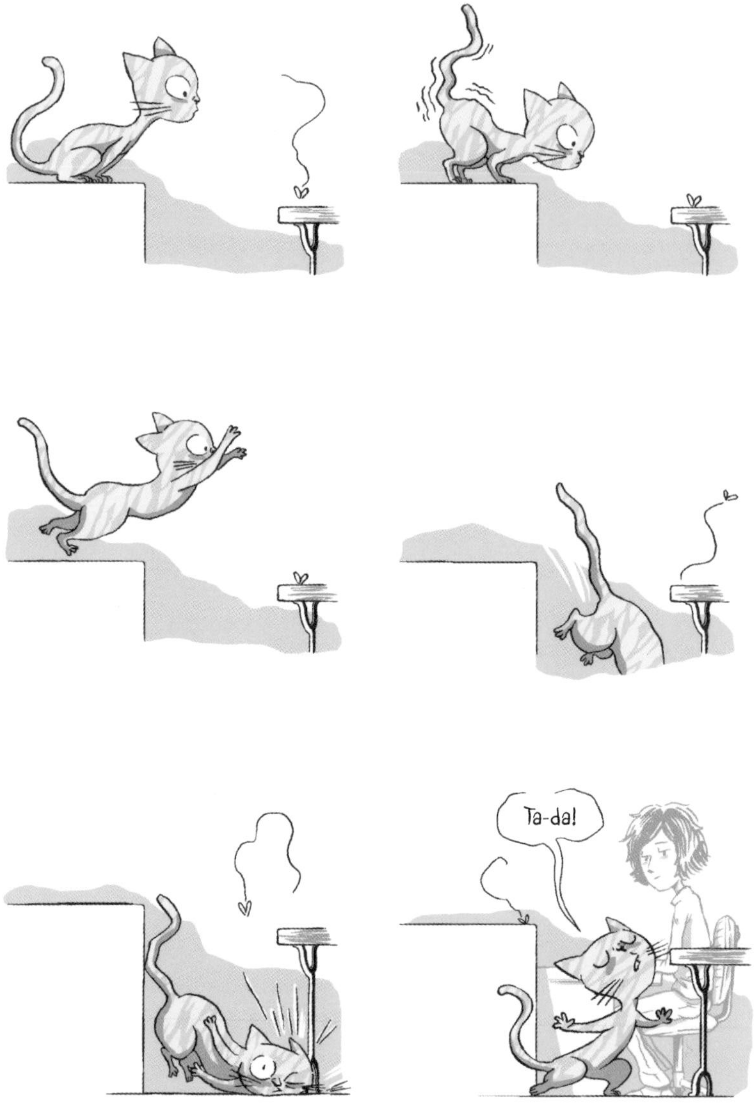
Ta-da!

Madame ponders

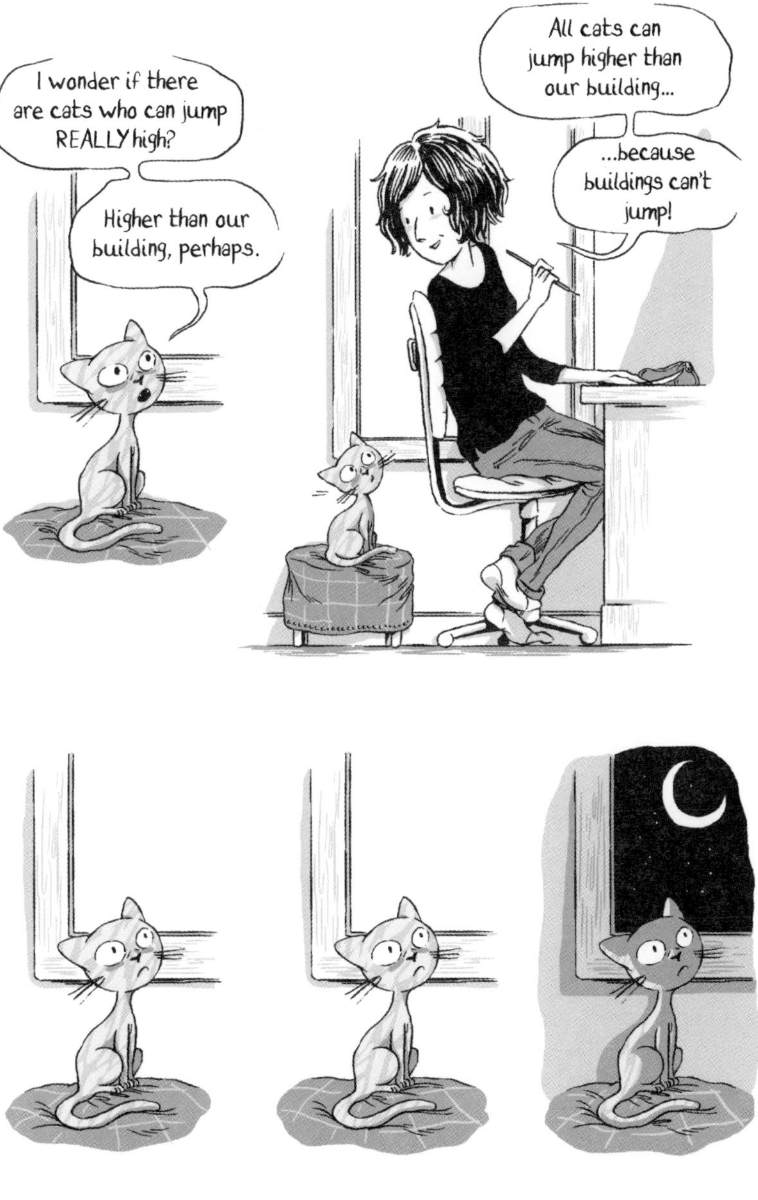

I wonder if there are cats who can jump REALLY high?
Higher than our building, perhaps.
All cats can jump higher than our building...
...because buildings can't jump!

Madame slashes

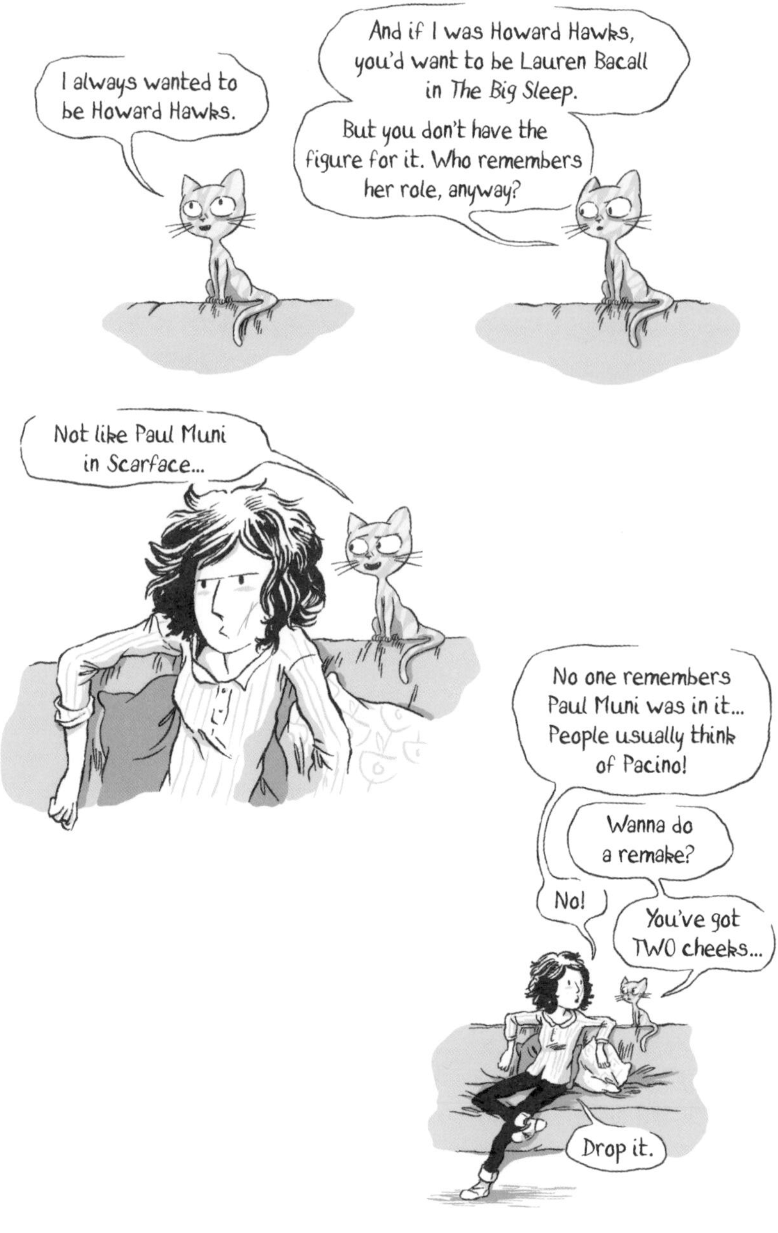
I always wanted to be Howard Hawks.
And if I was Howard Hawks, you'd want to be Lauren Bacall in *The Big Sleep*.
But you don't have the figure for it. Who remembers her role, anyway?
Not like Paul Muni in *Scarface*...
No one remembers Paul Muni was in it... People usually think of Pacino!
Wanna do a remake?
No!
You've got TWO cheeks...
Drop it.

Madame terrifies

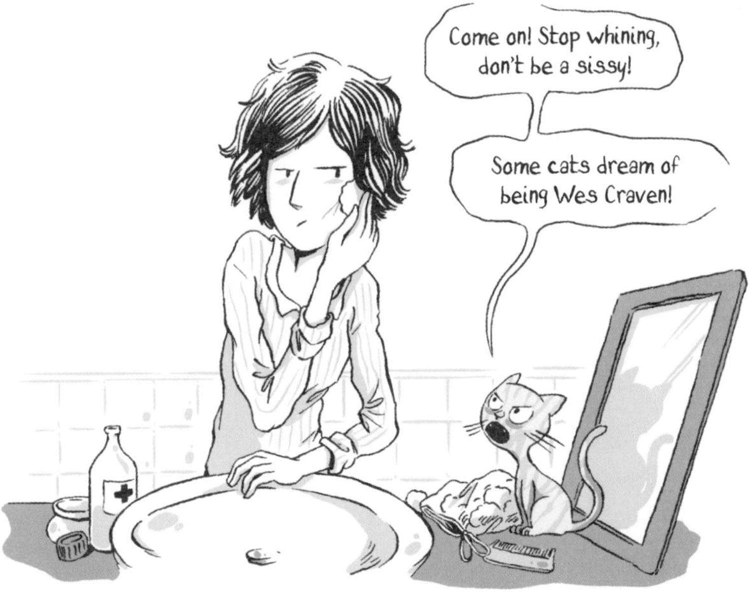
Come on! Stop whining, don't be a sissy!
Some cats dream of being Wes Craven!

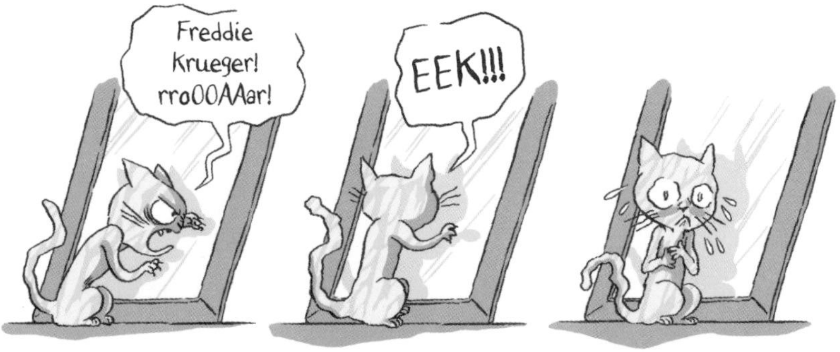
Freddie Krueger! rroOOAAar!
EEK!!!

Madame annotates

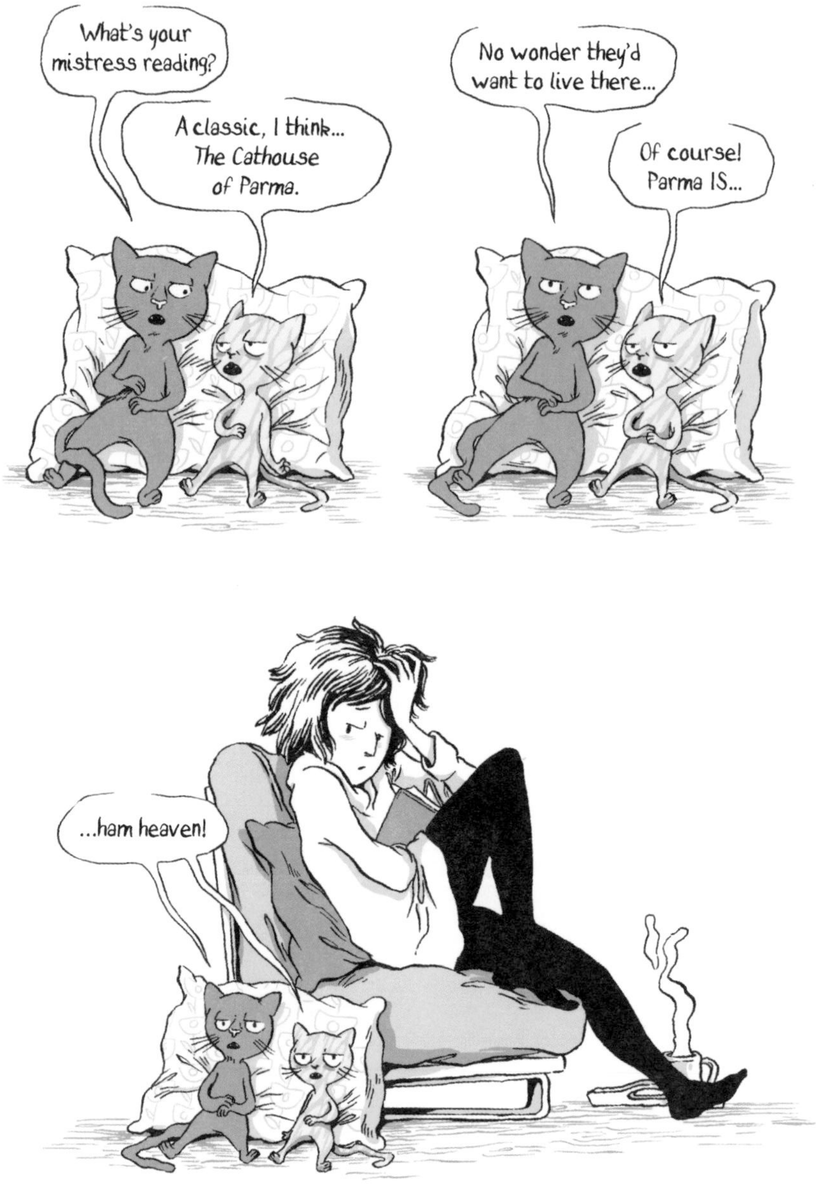
What's your mistress reading?
A classic, I think... The Cathouse of Parma.
No wonder they'd want to live there...
Of course! Parma IS...
...ham heaven!

Madame reflects

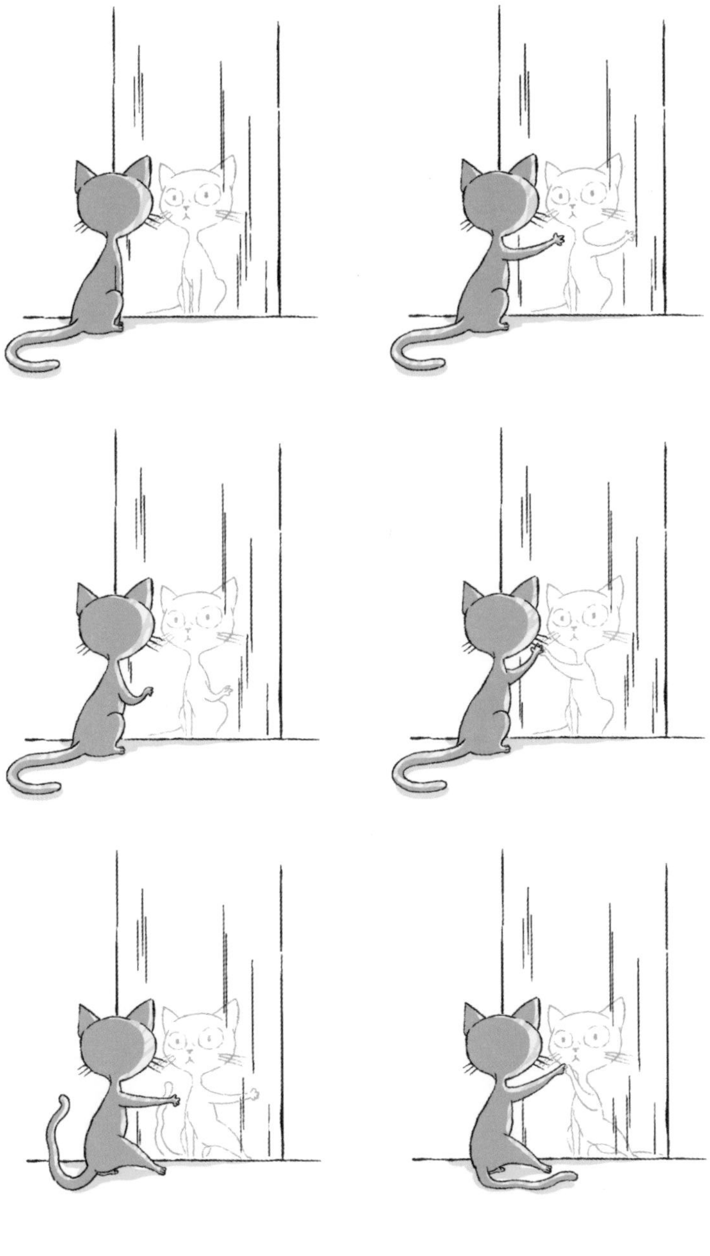

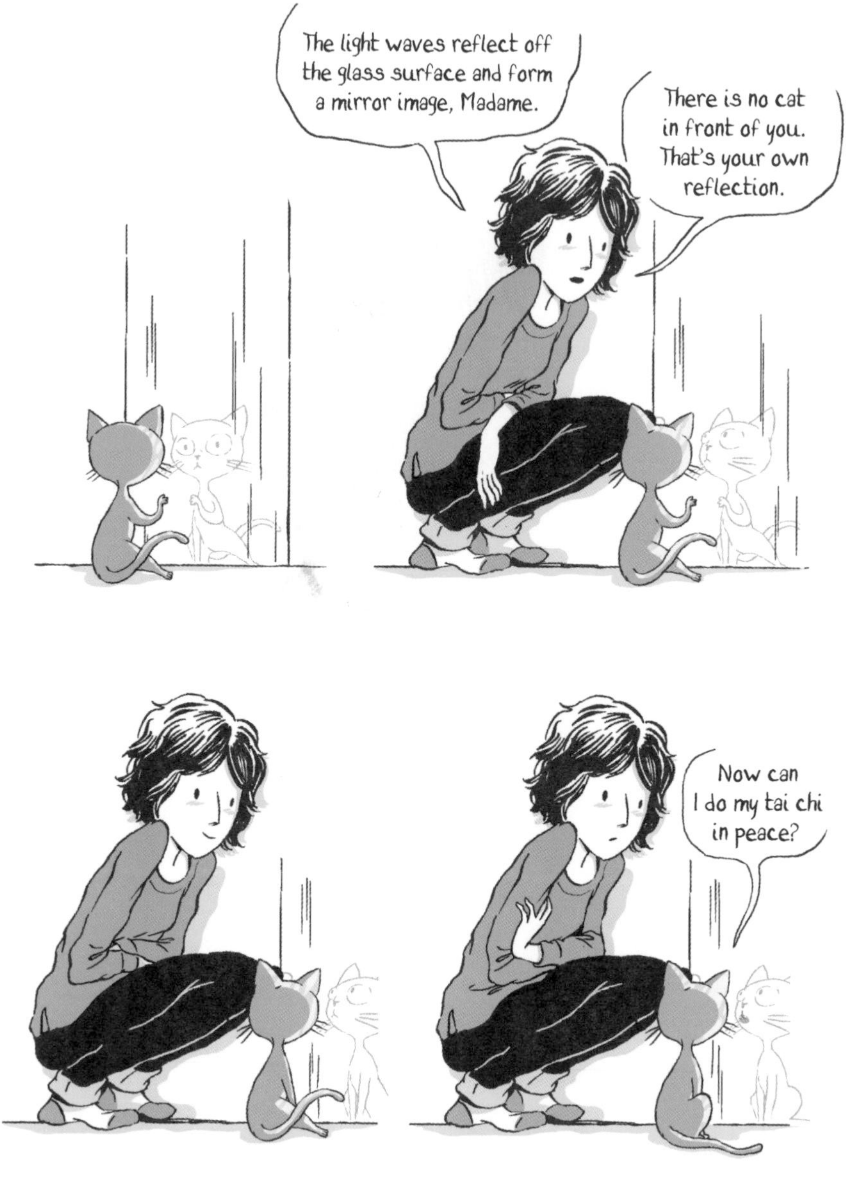
The light waves reflect off the glass surface and form a mirror image, Madame.
There is no cat in front of you. That's your own reflection.
Now can I do my tai chi in peace?

Madame matures

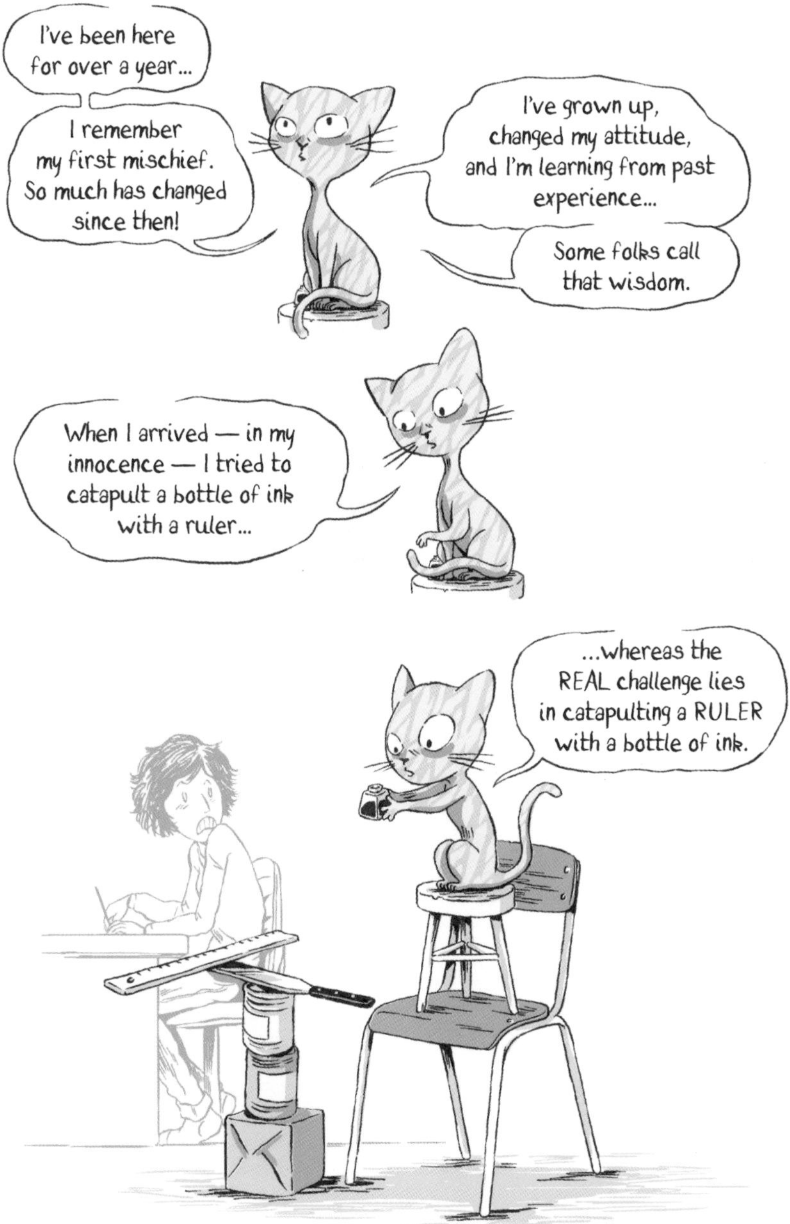

I've been here for over a year...
I remember my first mischief. So much has changed since then!
I've grown up, changed my attitude, and I'm learning from past experience...
Some folks call that wisdom.
When I arrived — in my innocence — I tried to catapult a bottle of ink with a ruler...
...whereas the REAL challenge lies in catapulting a RULER with a bottle of ink.

Madame inquires

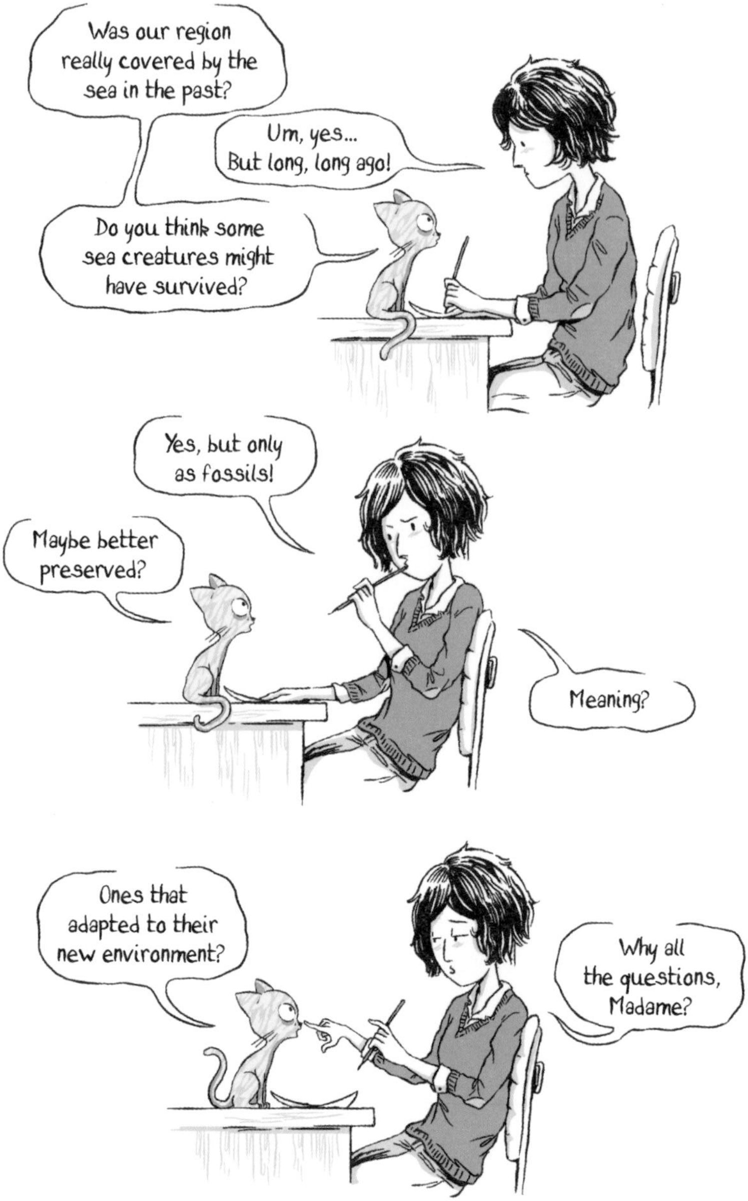

Was our region really covered by the sea in the past?
Um, yes... But long, long ago!
Do you think some sea creatures might have survived?
Yes, but only as fossils!
Maybe better preserved?
Meaning?
Ones that adapted to their new environment?
Why all the questions, Madame?

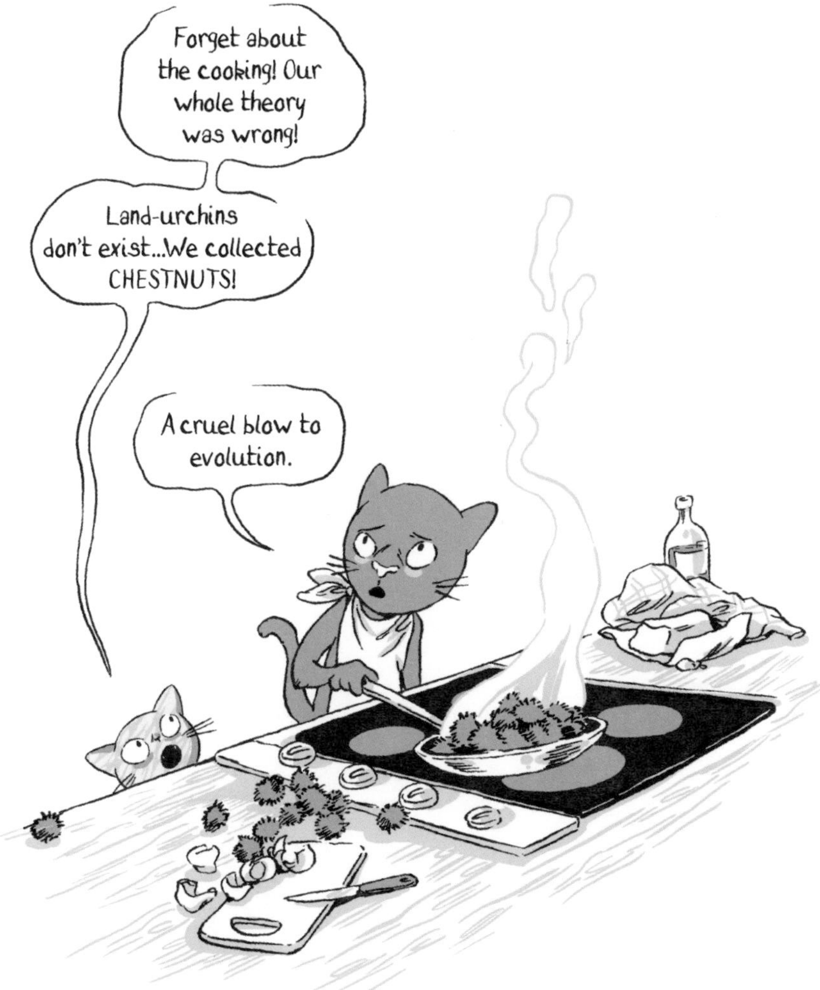
Forget about the cooking! Our whole theory was wrong!
Land-urchins don't exist...We collected CHESTNUTS!
A cruel blow to evolution.

Madame waters

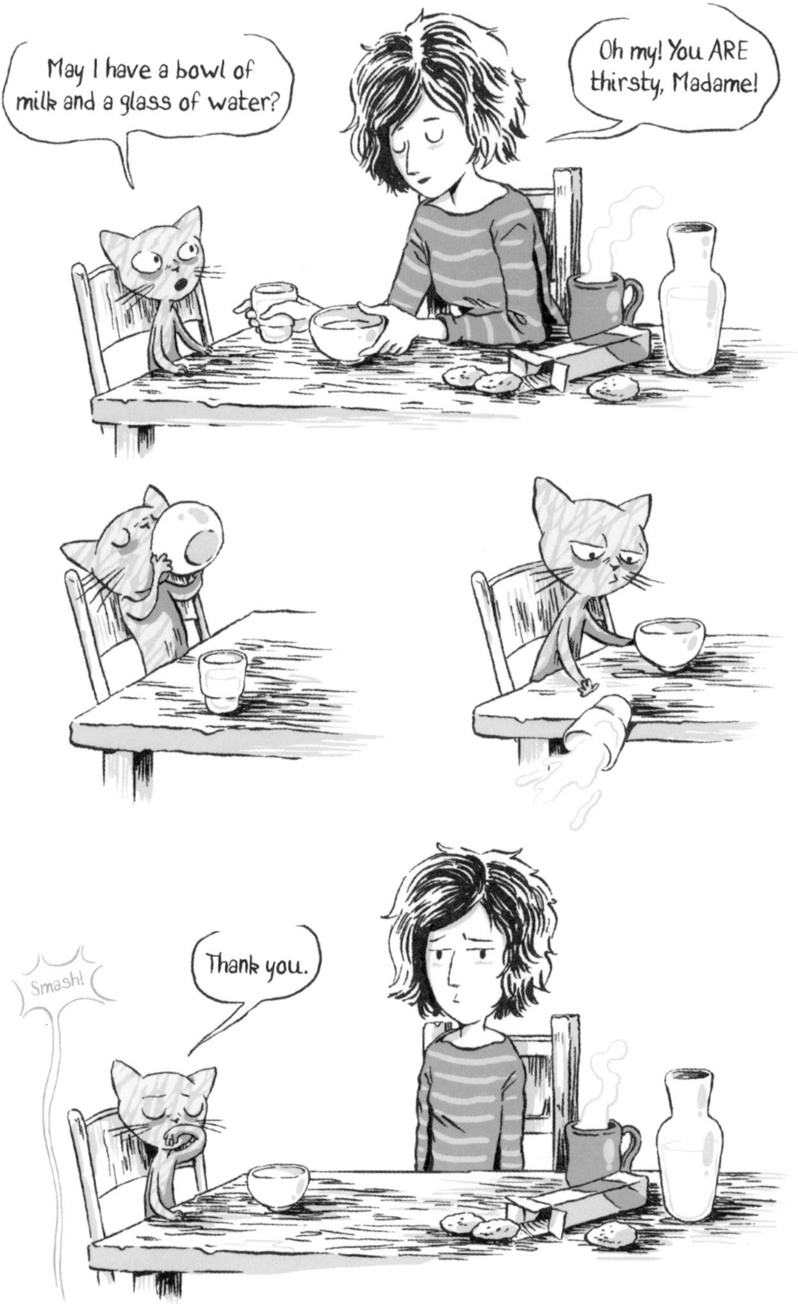
May I have a bowl of milk and a glass of water?
Oh my! You ARE thirsty, Madame!
Smash!
Thank you.

Madame performs

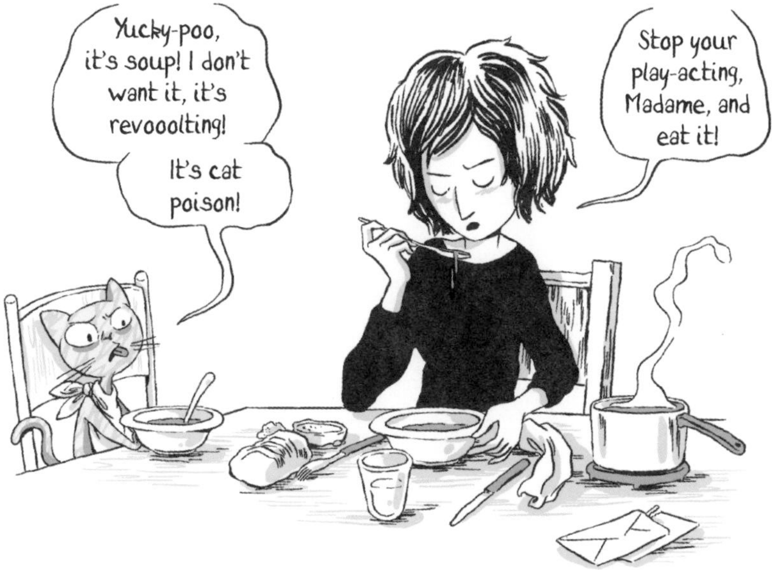
Yucky-poo, it's soup! I don't want it, it's revooolting!
It's cat poison!
Stop your play-acting, Madame, and eat it!

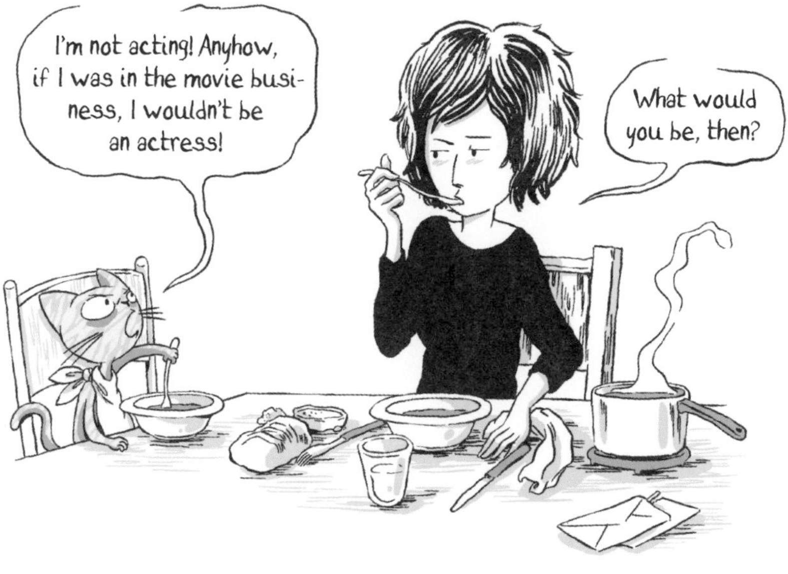
I'm not acting! Anyhow, if I was in the movie busi-ness, I wouldn't be an actress!
What would you be, then?

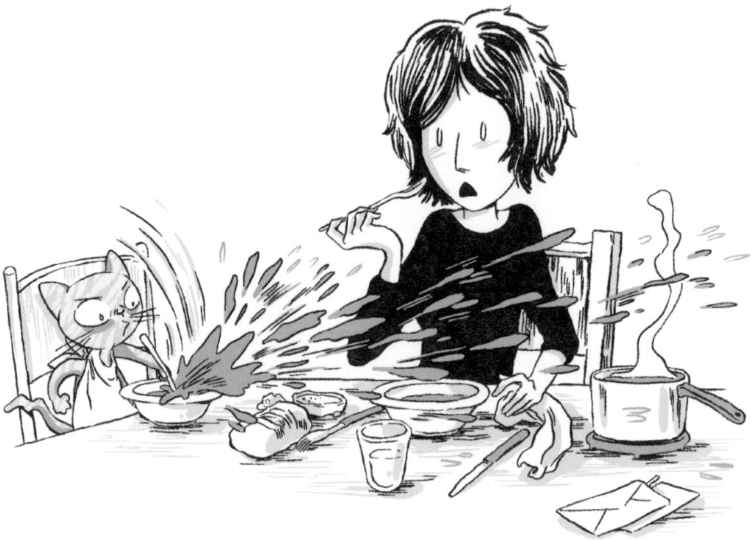

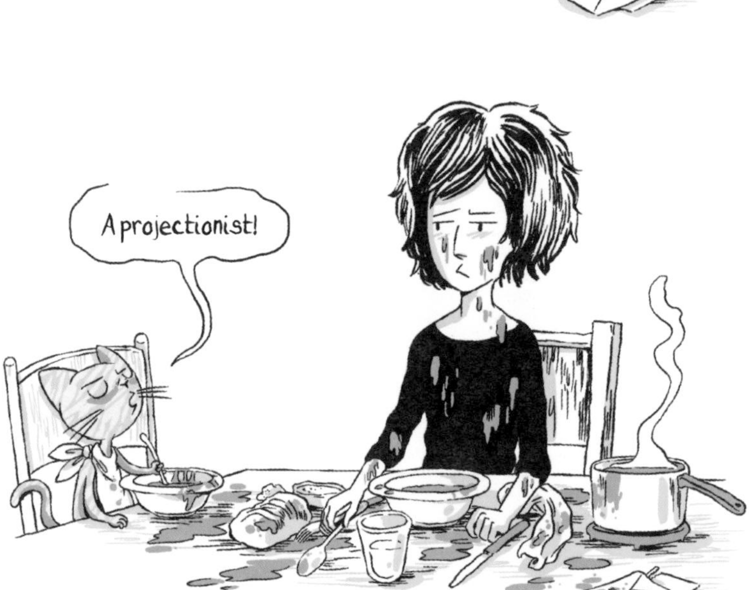
A projectionist!

Madame meditates

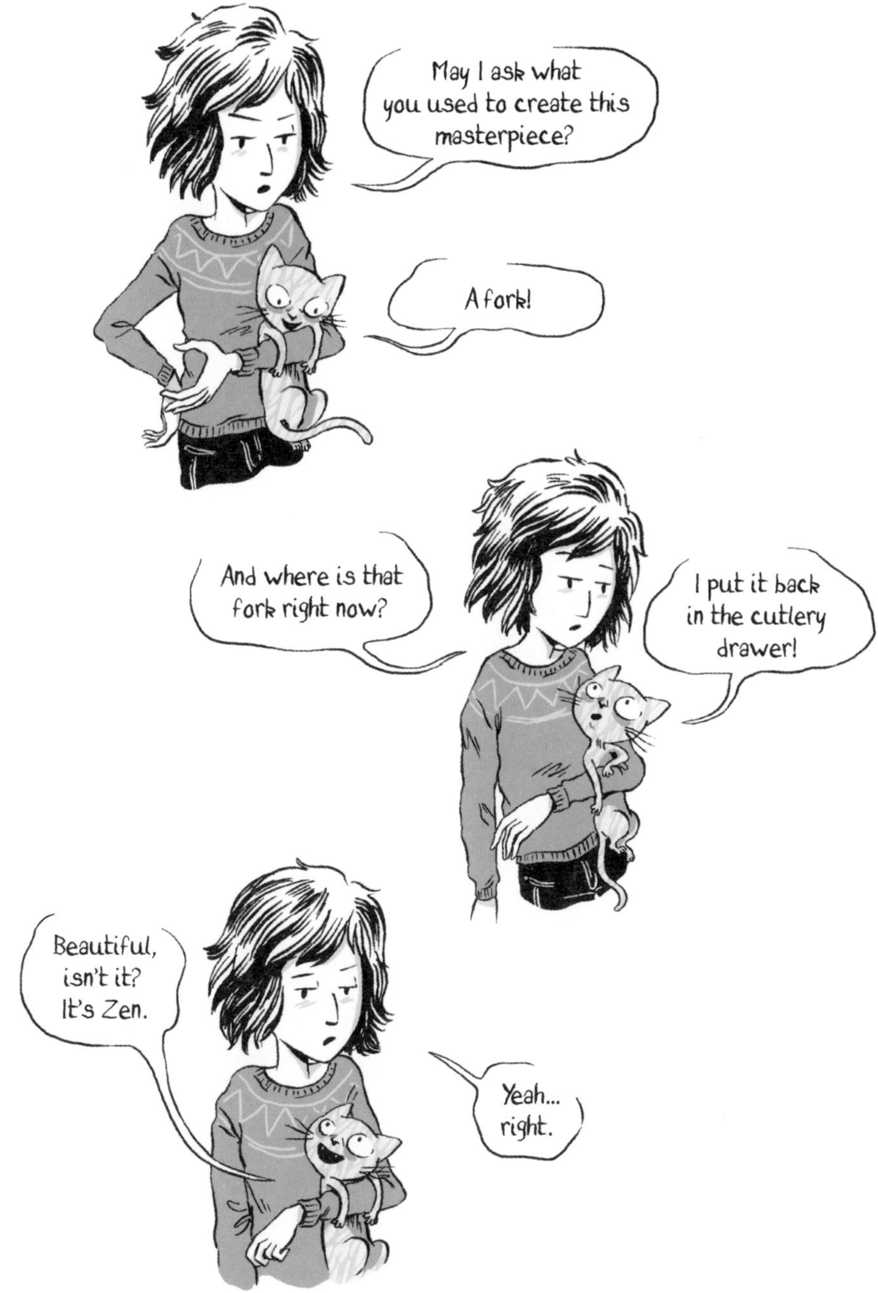
May I ask what you used to create this masterpiece?
A fork!
And where is that fork right now?
I put it back in the cutlery drawer!
Beautiful, isn't it? It's Zen.
Yeah... right.

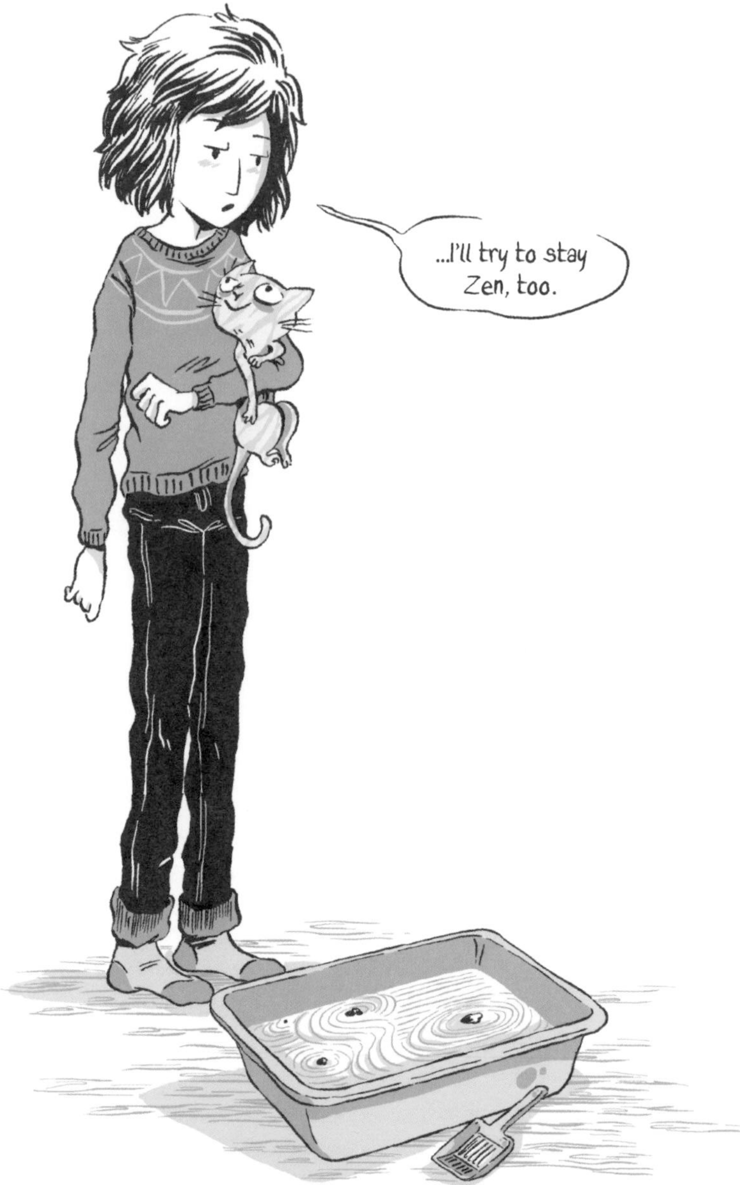
...I'll try to stay Zen, too.

Madame proposes

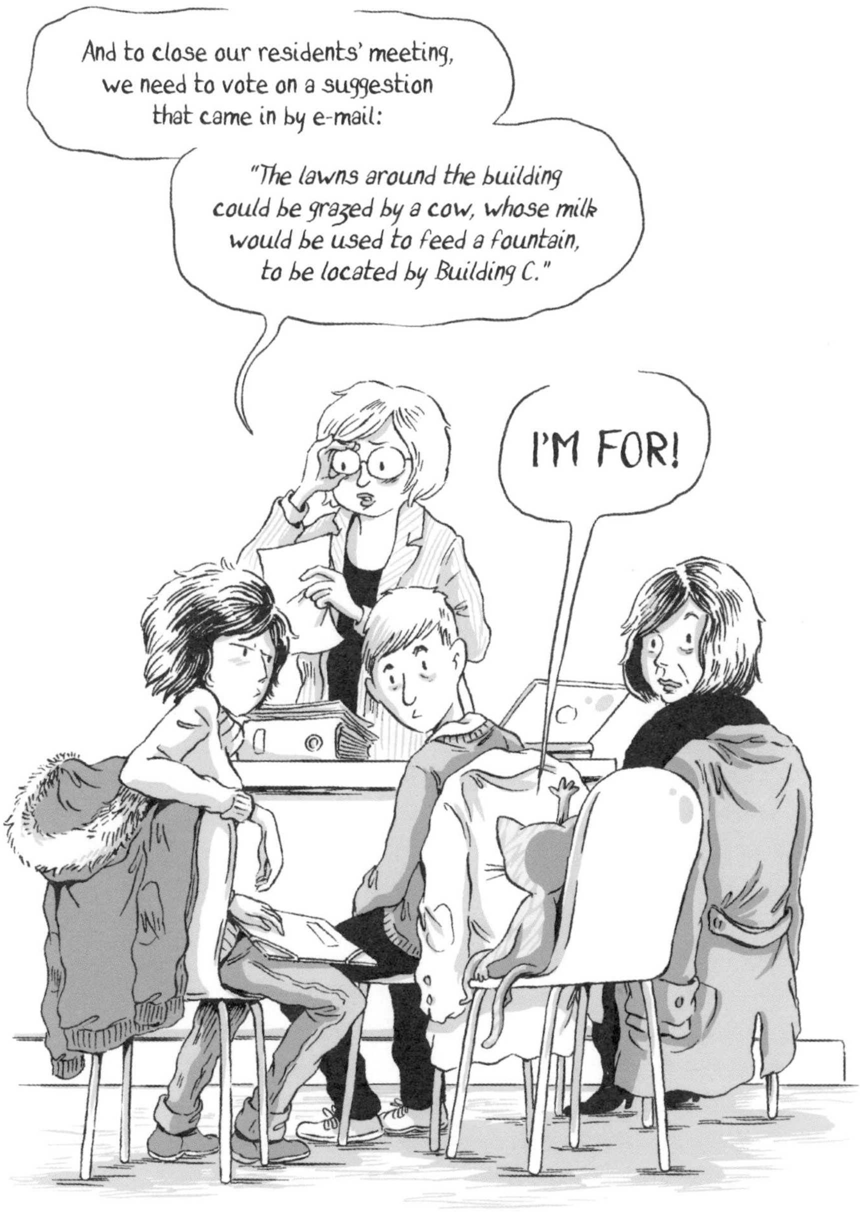

And to close our residents' meeting, we need to vote on a suggestion that came in by e-mail:
"The lawns around the building could be grazed by a cow, whose milk would be used to feed a fountain, to be located by Building C."
I'M FOR!

Madame shoves

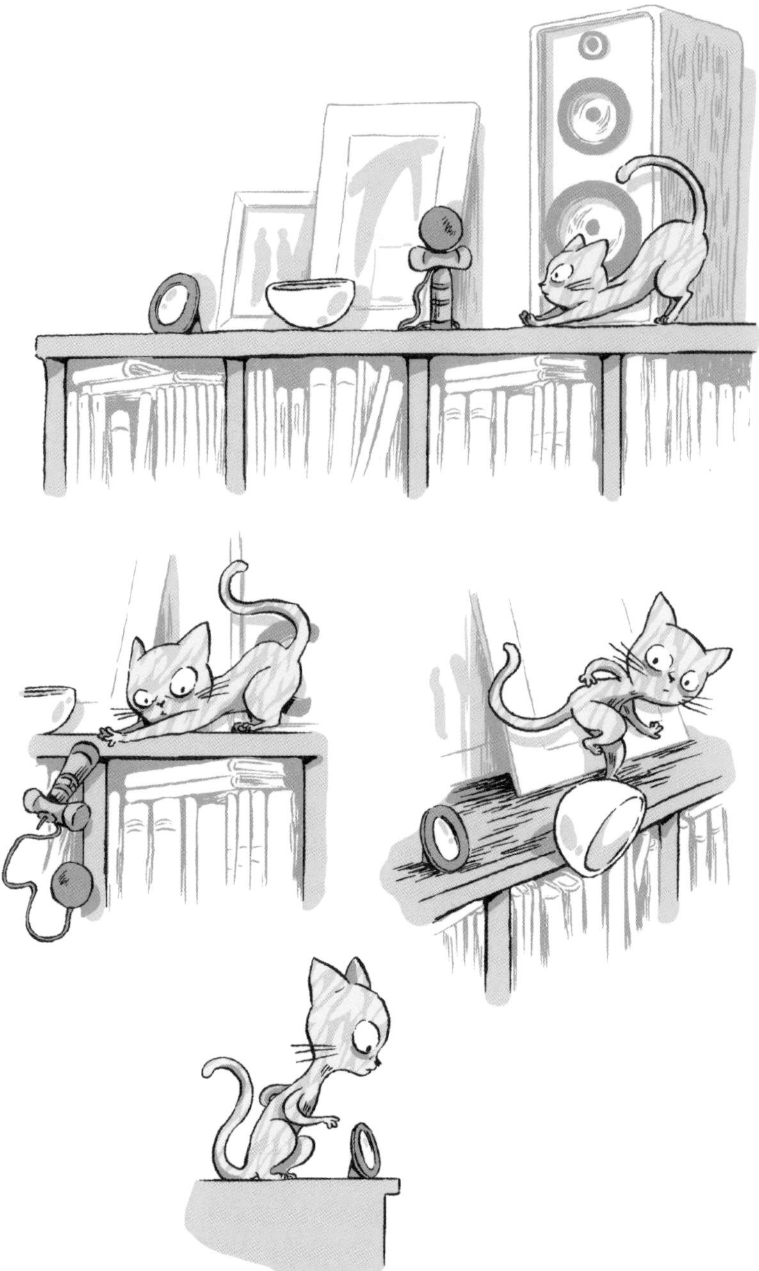

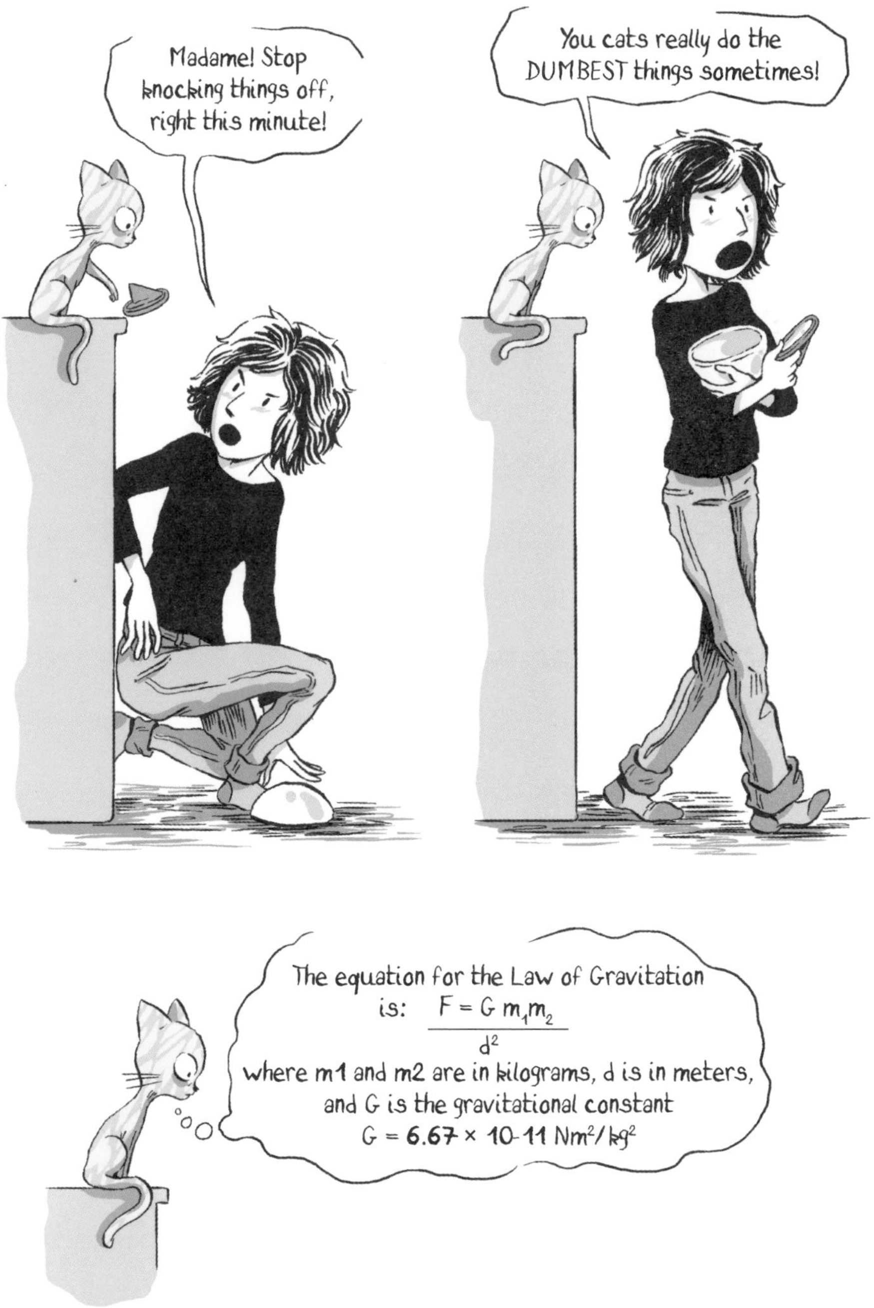
Madame! Stop knocking things off, right this minute!
You cats really do the DUMBEST things sometimes!
The equation for the Law of Gravitation is: $F = \frac{G m_1 m_2}{d^2}$
where m1 and m2 are in kilograms, d is in meters, and G is the gravitational constant
G = **6.67** × **10-11** Nm^2/kg^2

Madame proverbializes

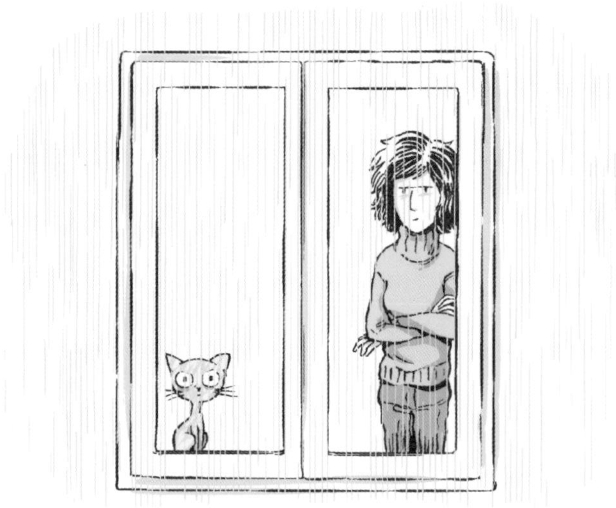

A chill wind outside, and down the rain pours,

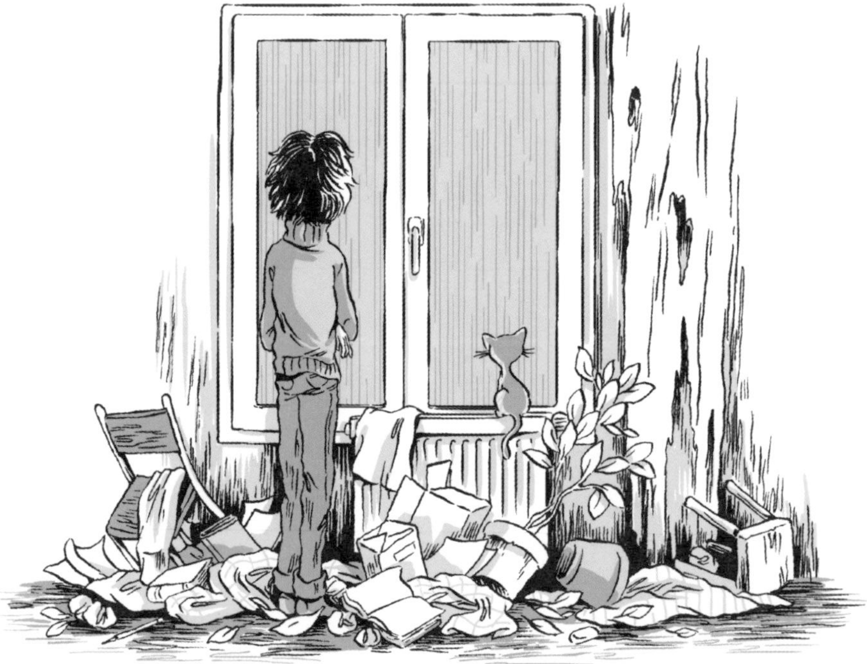

You will face the Apocalypse indoors.

Madame answers

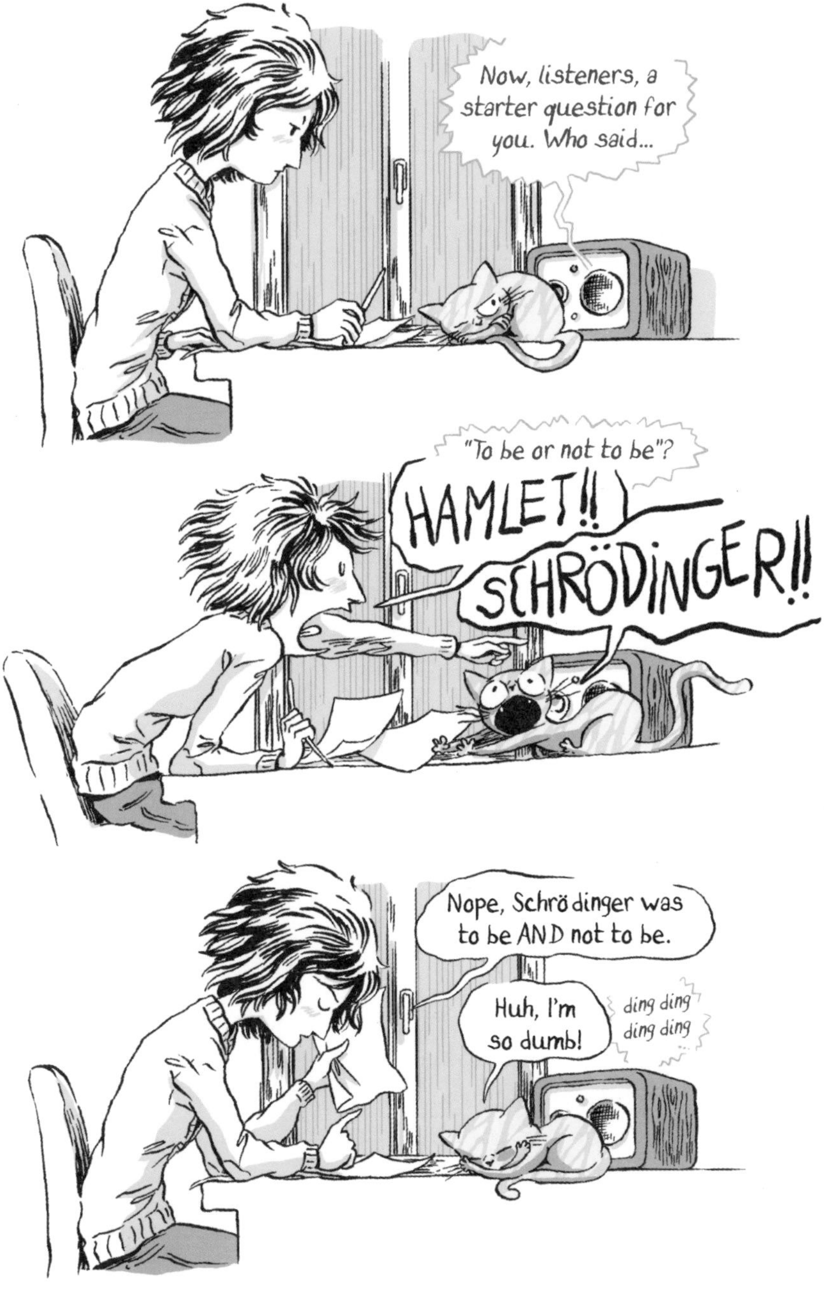
Now, listeners, a starter question for you. Who said...
"To be or not to be"?
HAMLET!!
SCHRÖDINGER!!
Nope, Schrödinger was to be AND not to be.
Huh, I'm so dumb!
ding ding ding ding

Madame pilots

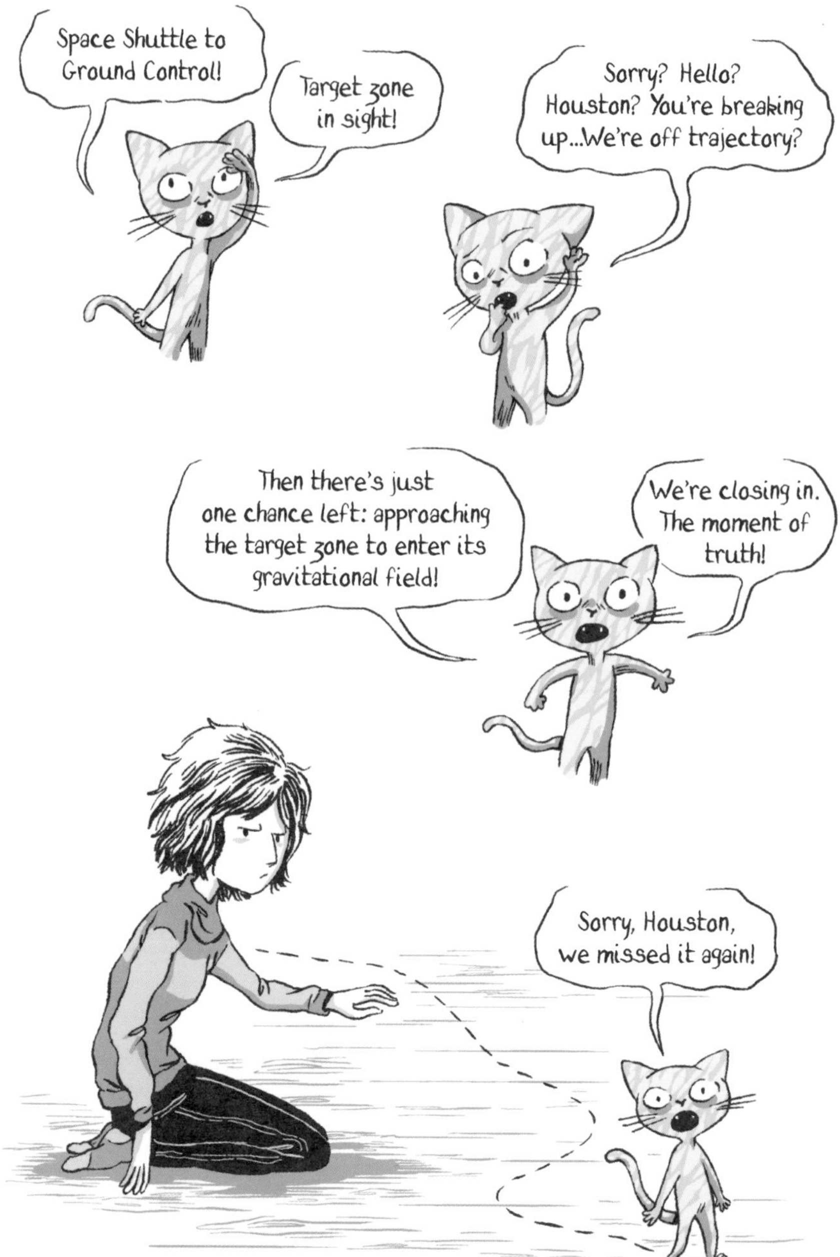
Space Shuttle to Ground Control!
Target zone in sight!
Sorry? Hello? Houston? You're breaking up...We're off trajectory?
Then there's just one chance left: approaching the target zone to enter its gravitational field!
We're closing in. The moment of truth!
Sorry, Houston, we missed it again!

Madame harpoons

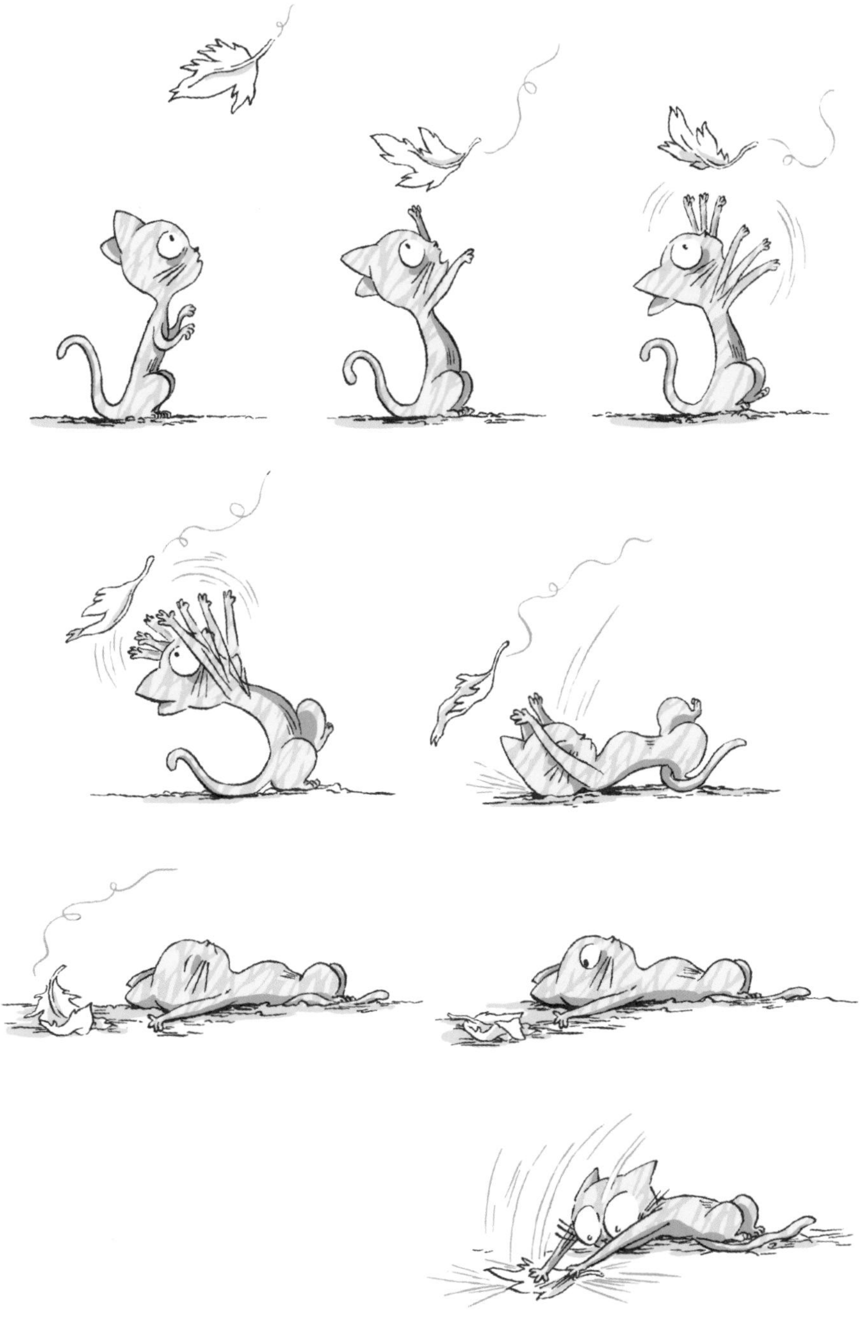

Madame preens

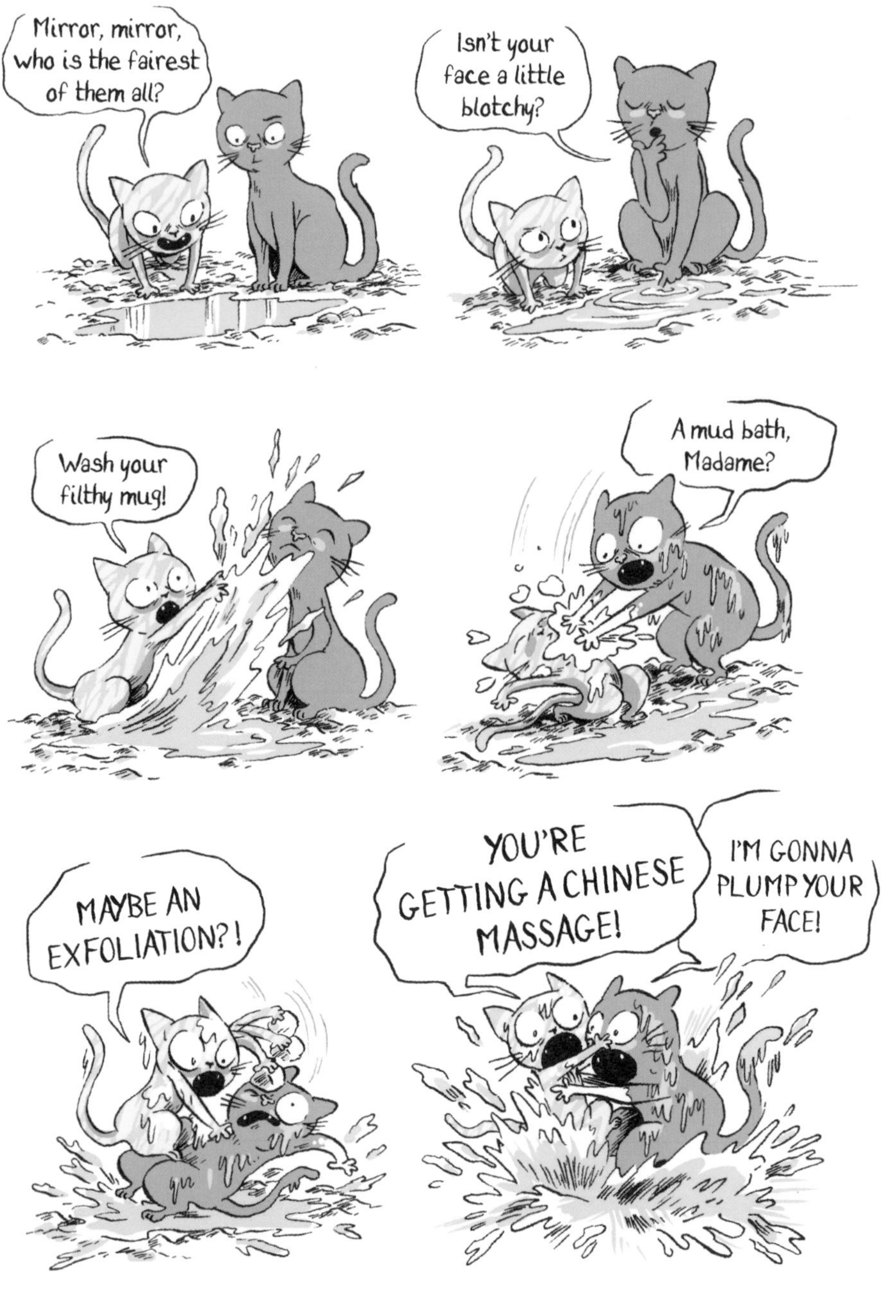
Mirror, mirror, who is the fairest of them all?
Isn't your face a little blotchy?
Wash your filthy mug!
A mud bath, Madame?
MAYBE AN EXFOLIATION?!
YOU'RE GETTING A CHINESE MASSAGE!
I'M GONNA PLUMP YOUR FACE!

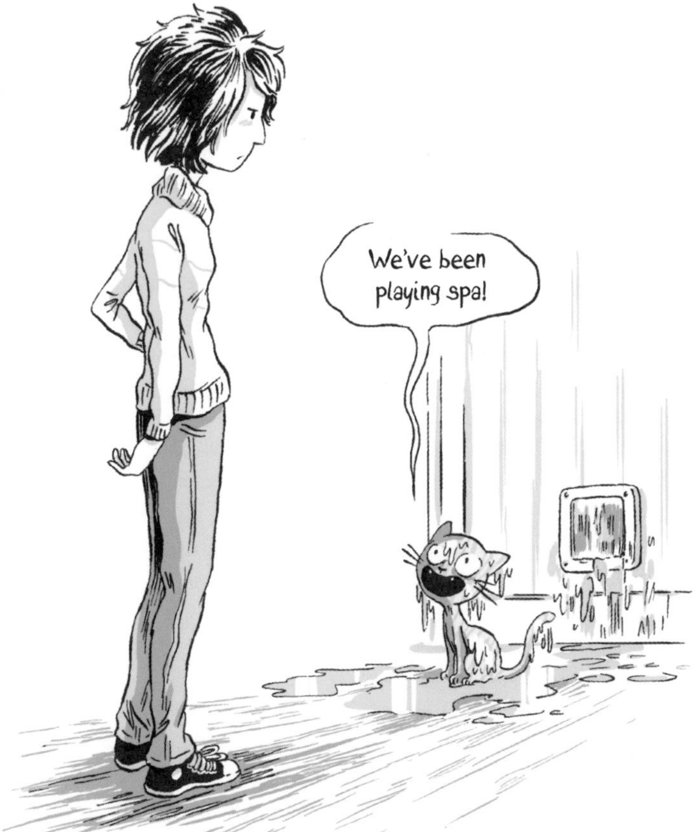
We've been playing spa!

Madame celebrates

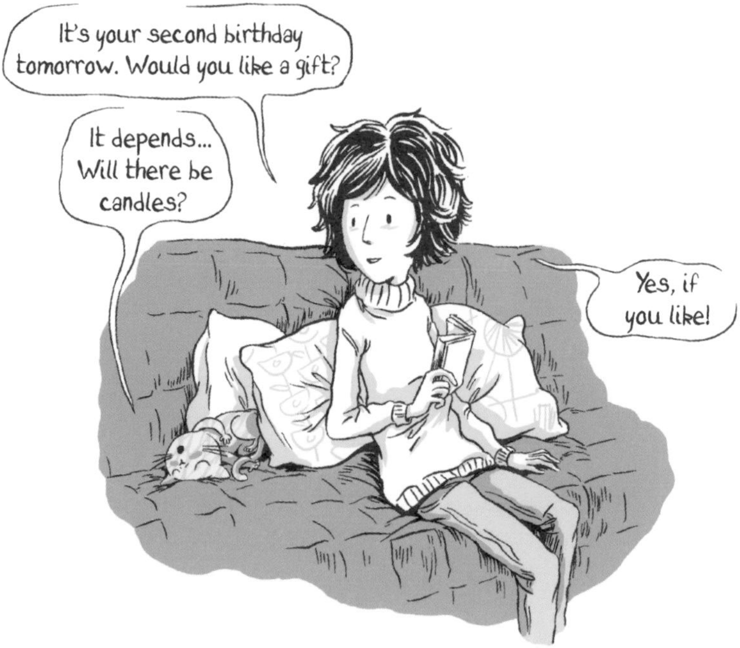
It's your second birthday tomorrow. Would you like a gift?
It depends... Will there be candles?
Yes, if you like!

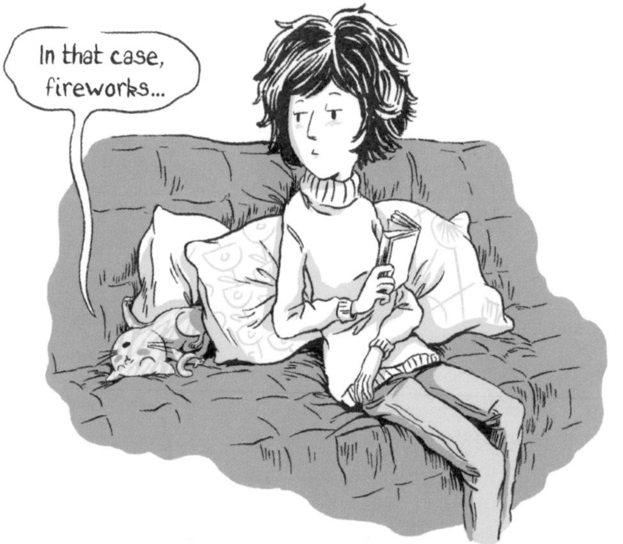
In that case, fireworks...

Madame panics

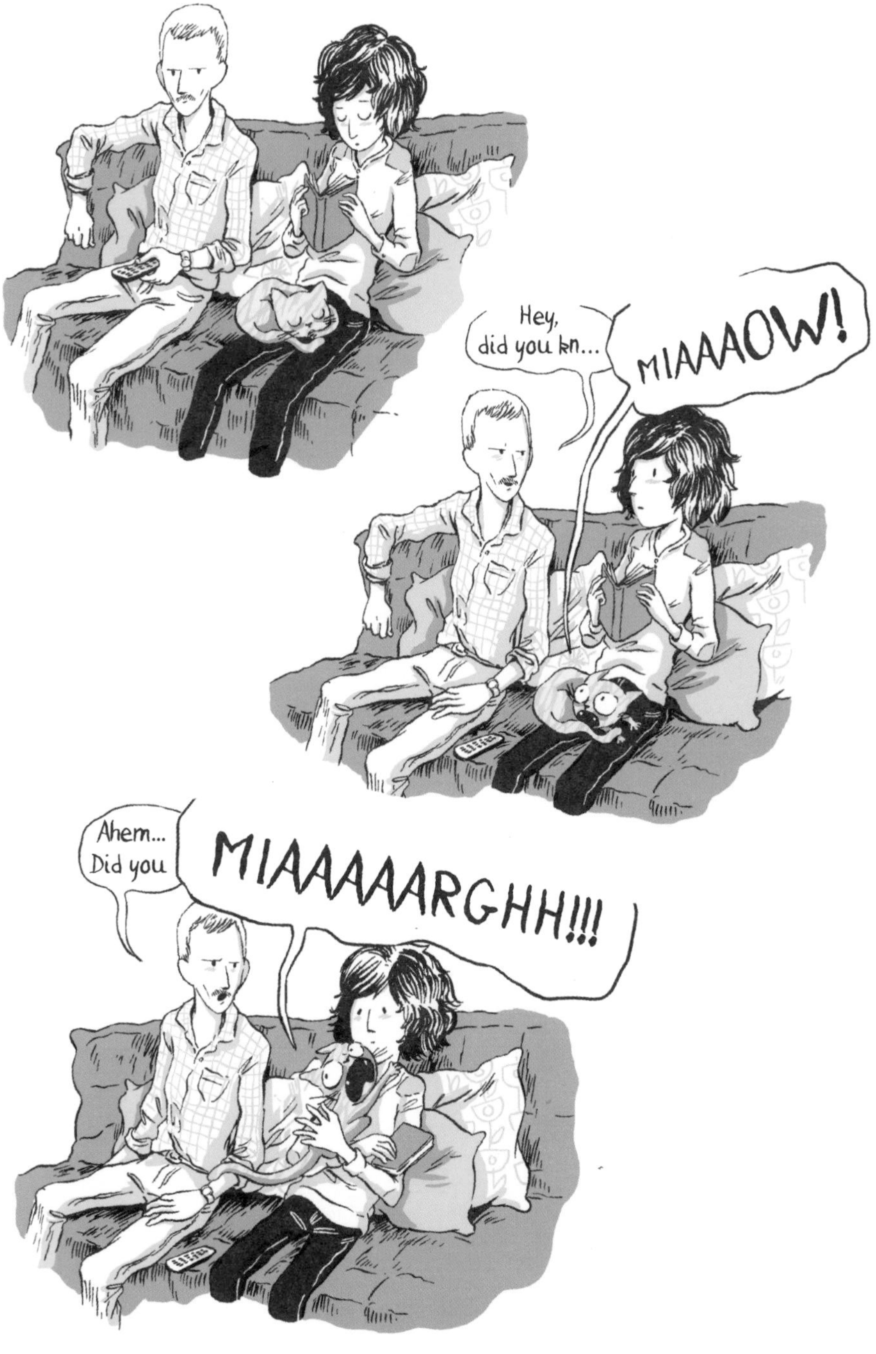
Hey, did you kn...
MIAAAOW!
Ahem... Did you
MIAAAAAARGHH!!!

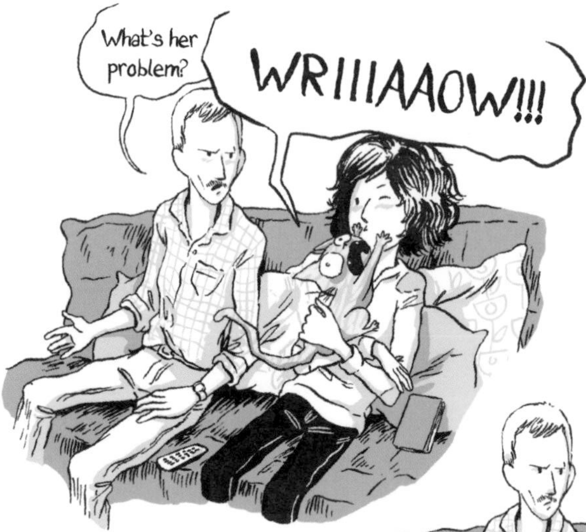
What's her problem?
WRIIIAAOW!!!

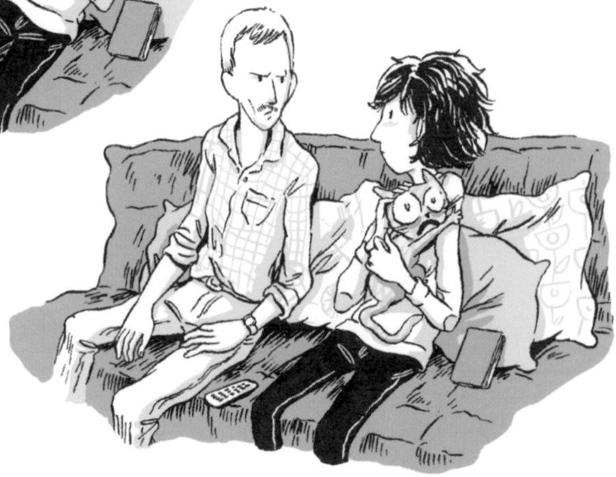

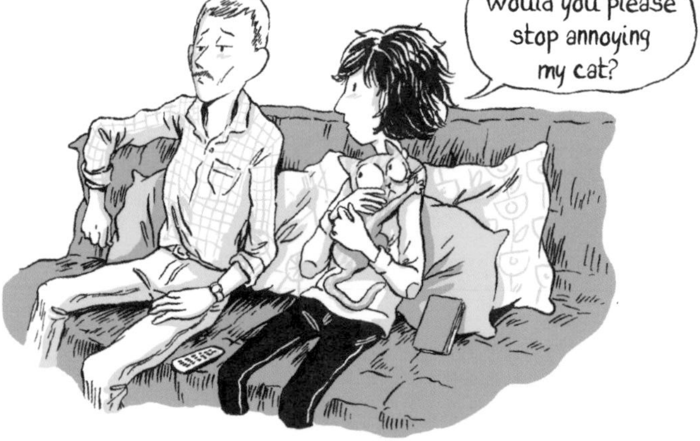
Would you please stop annoying my cat?

Madame stares

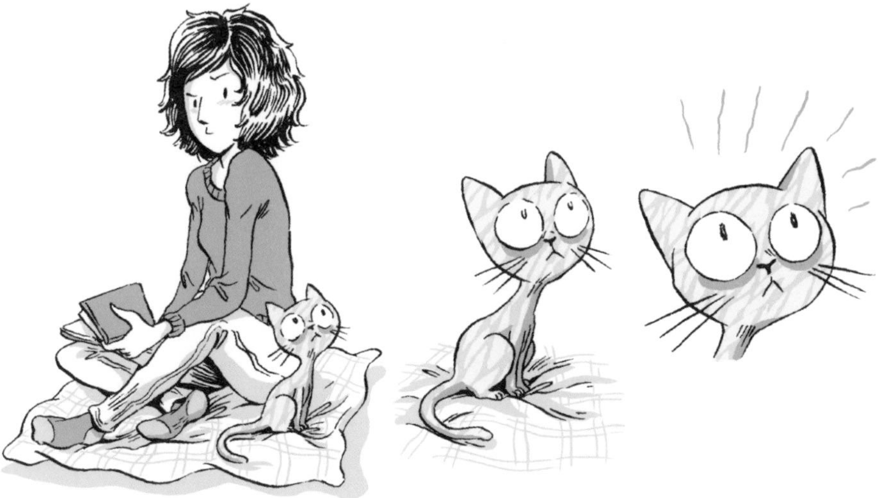

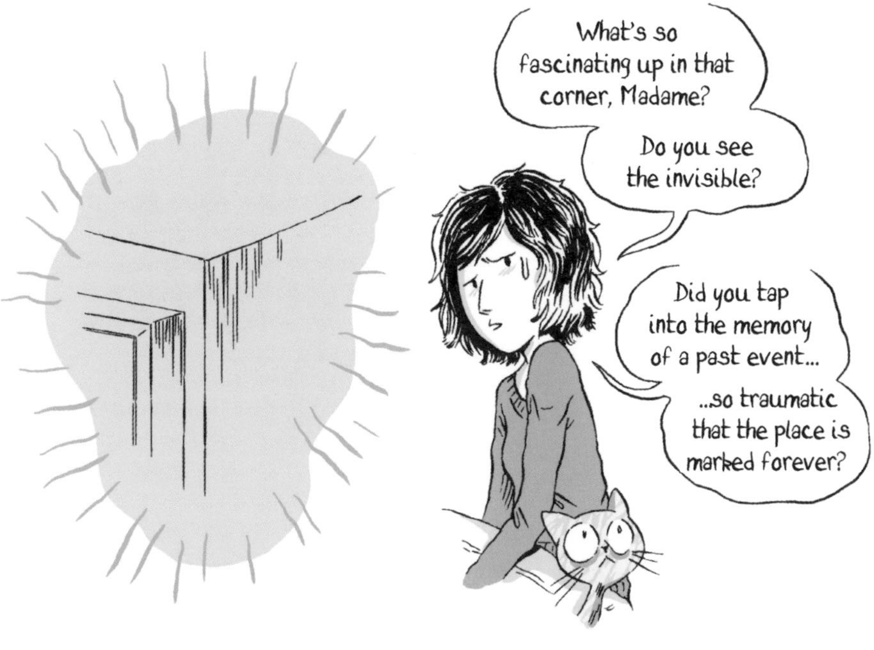
What's so fascinating up in that corner, Madame?
Do you see the invisible?
Did you tap into the memory of a past event...
...so traumatic that the place is marked forever?

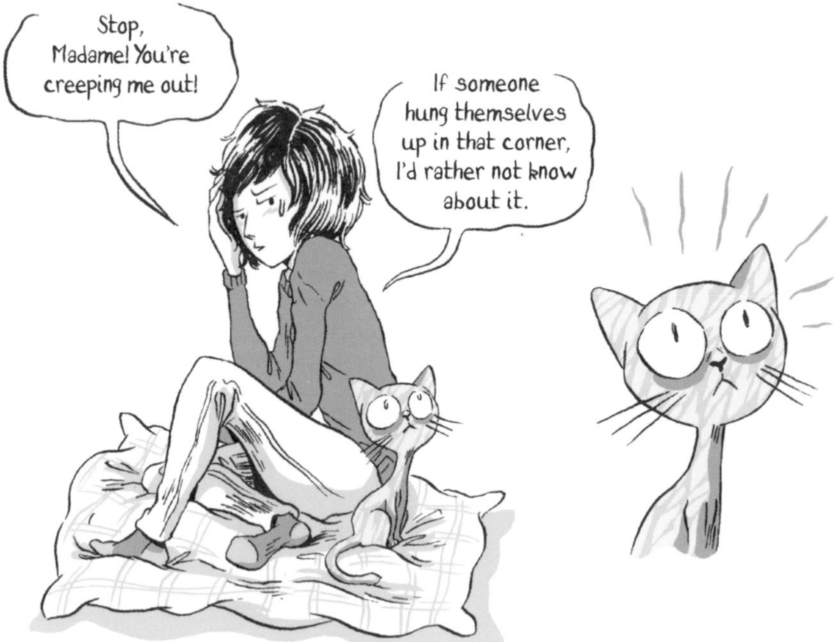
Stop, Madame! You're creeping me out!
If someone hung themselves up in that corner, I'd rather not know about it.

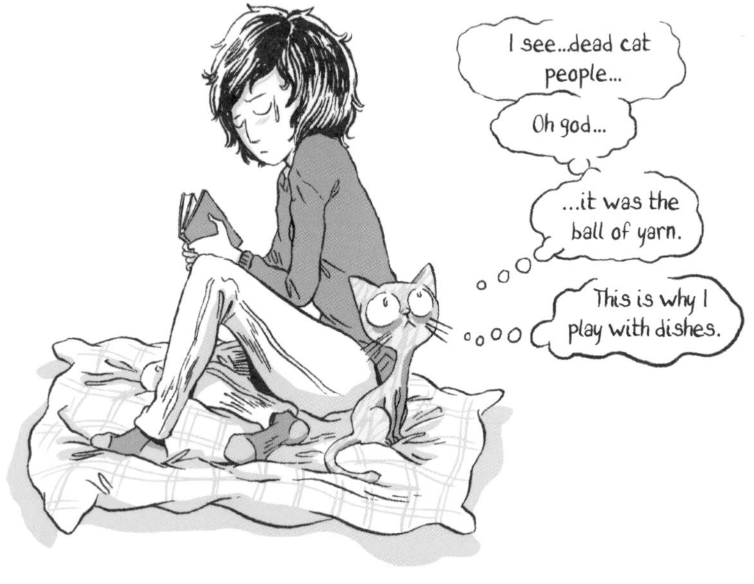
I see...dead cat people...
Oh god...
...it was the ball of yarn.
This is why I play with dishes.

Madame orders

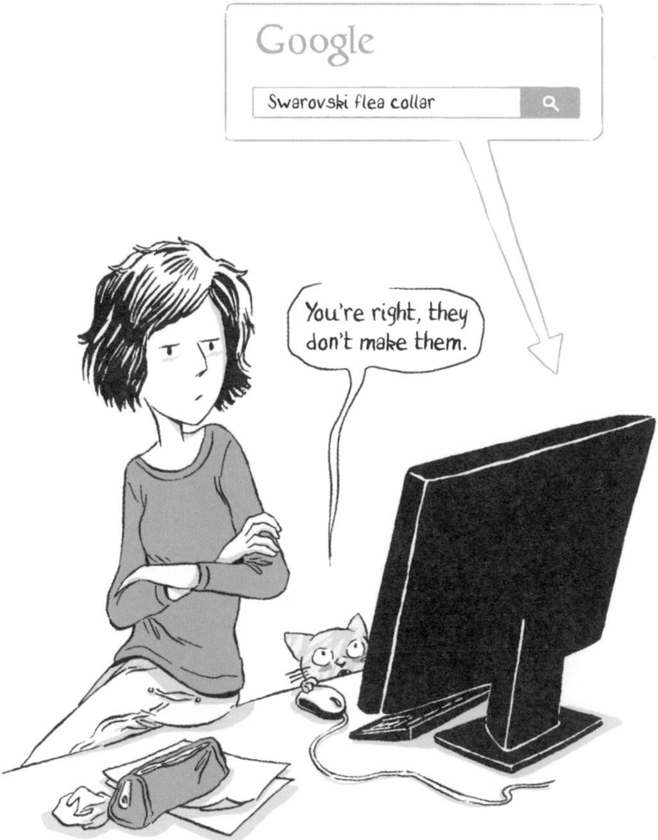
Google
Swarovski flea collar
You're right, they don't make them.

Madame spends

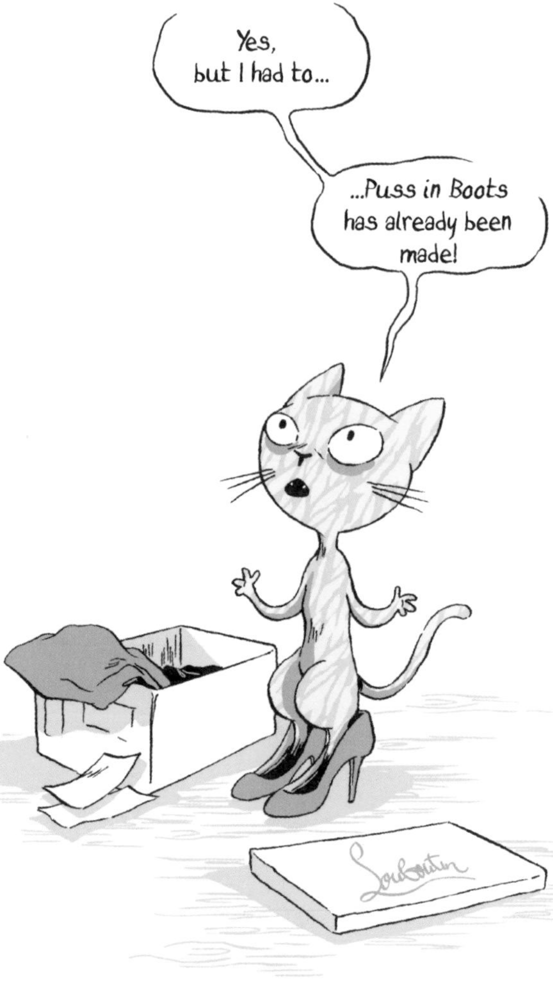

Yes, but I had to...
...Puss in Boots has already been made!

Madame opts

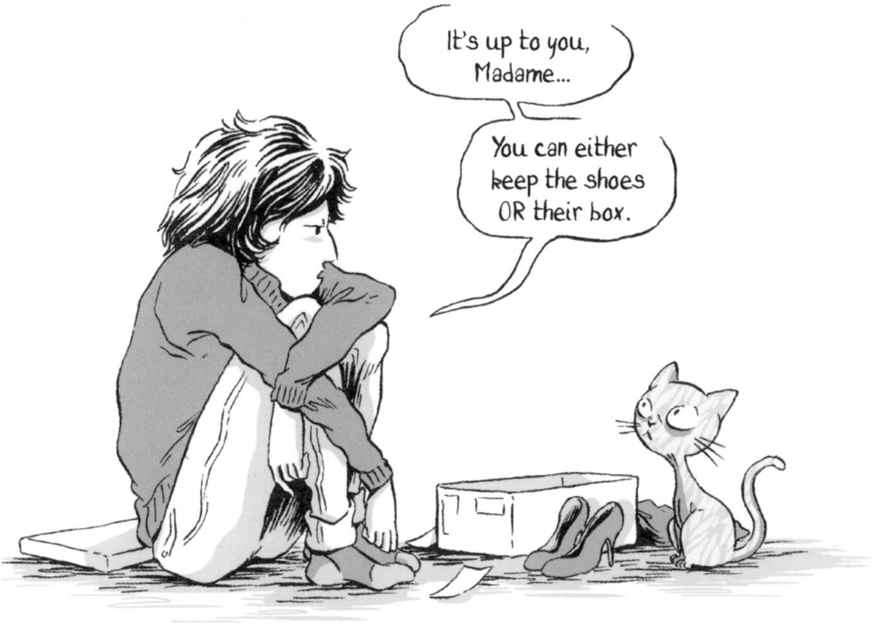
It's up to you, Madame...
You can either keep the shoes OR their box.

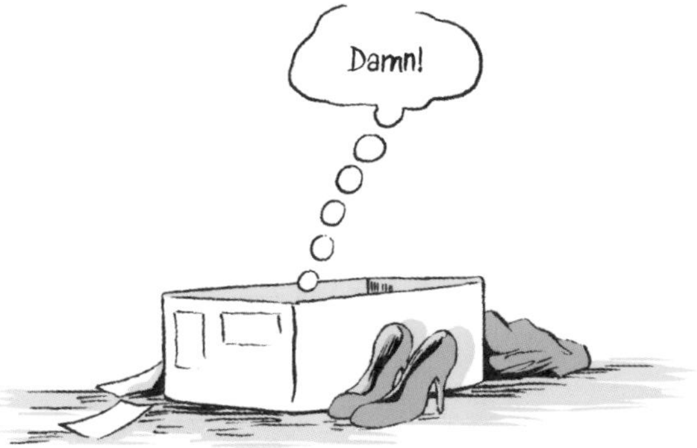
Damn!

Madame suffers

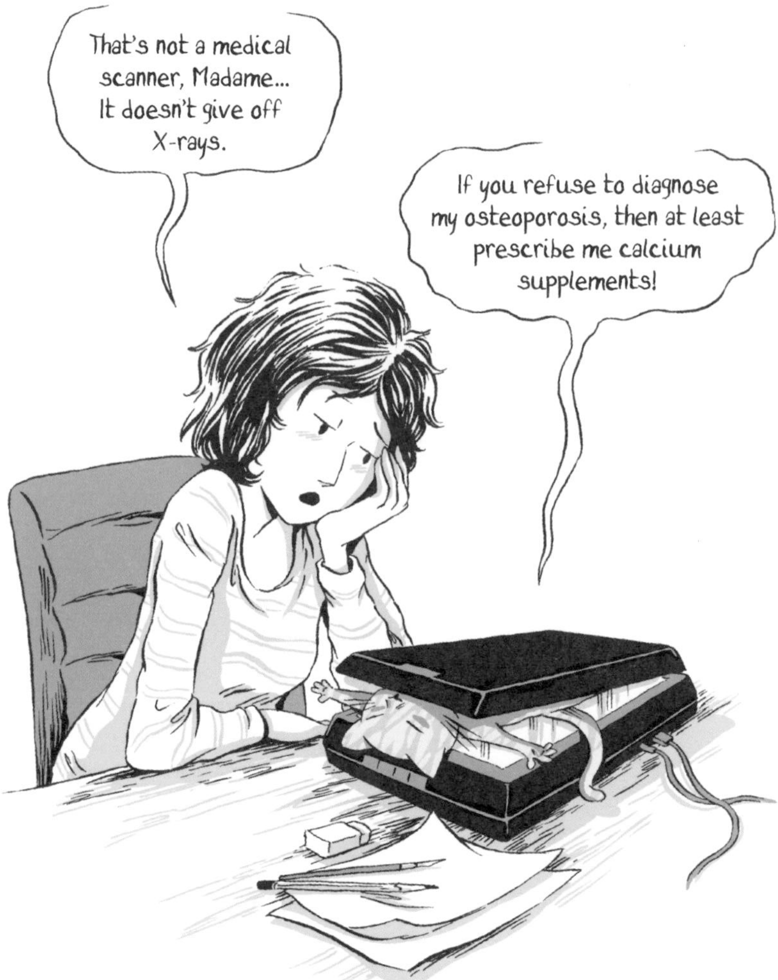
That's not a medical scanner, Madame... It doesn't give off X-rays.
If you refuse to diagnose my osteoporosis, then at least prescribe me calcium supplements!

Madame postures

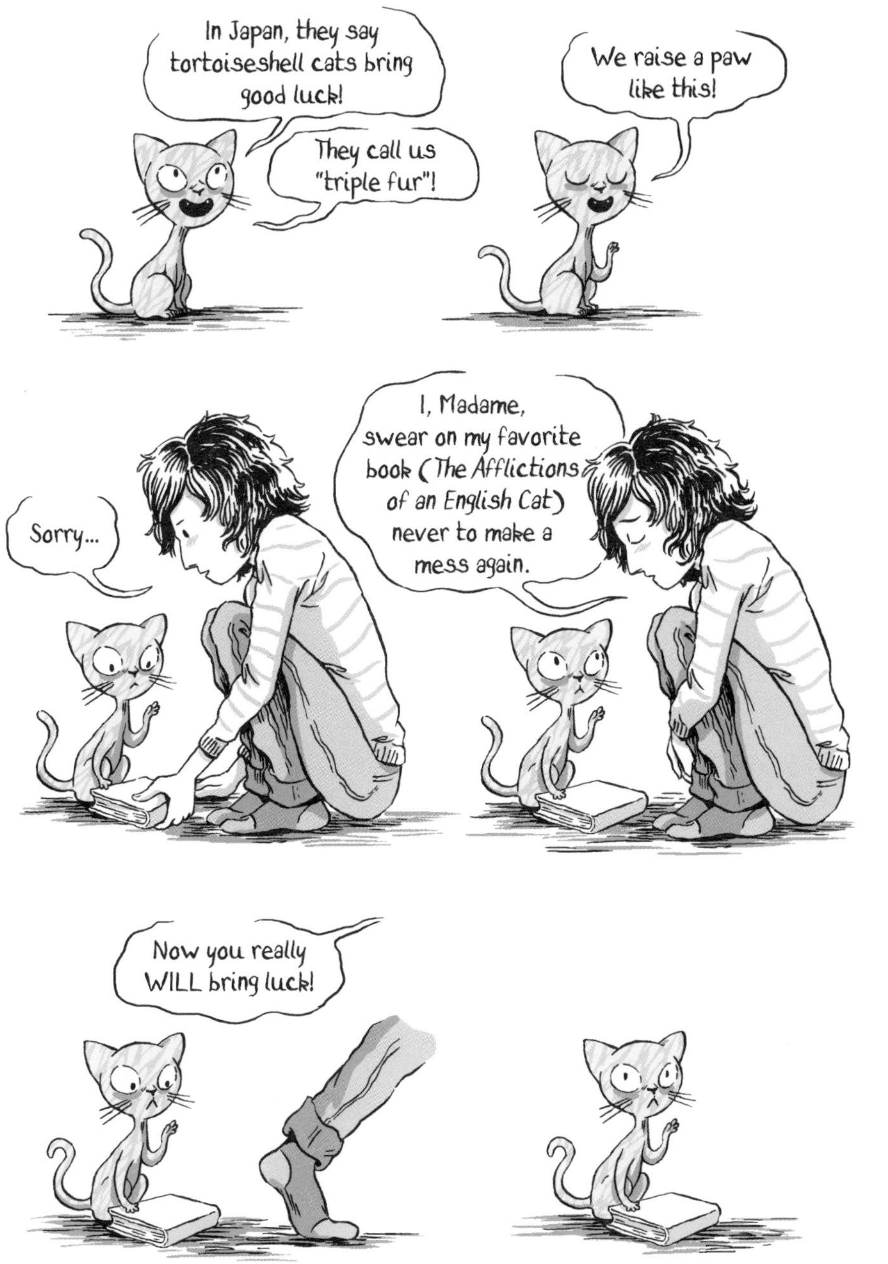

In Japan, they say tortoiseshell cats bring good luck!
They call us "triple fur"!
We raise a paw like this!
Sorry...
I, Madame, swear on my favorite book (*The Afflictions of an English Cat*) never to make a mess again.
Now you really WILL bring luck!

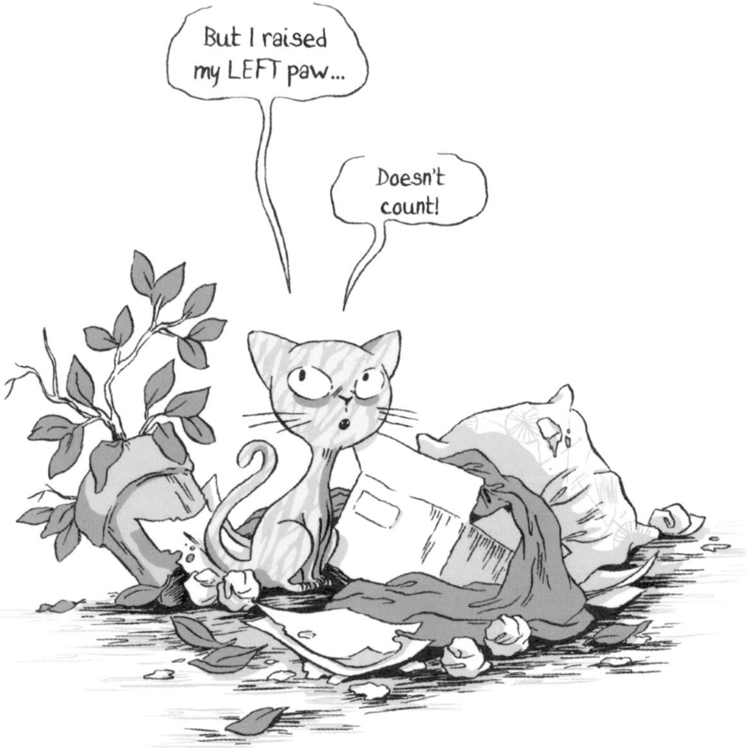
But I raised my LEFT paw...
Doesn't count!

Madame poaches

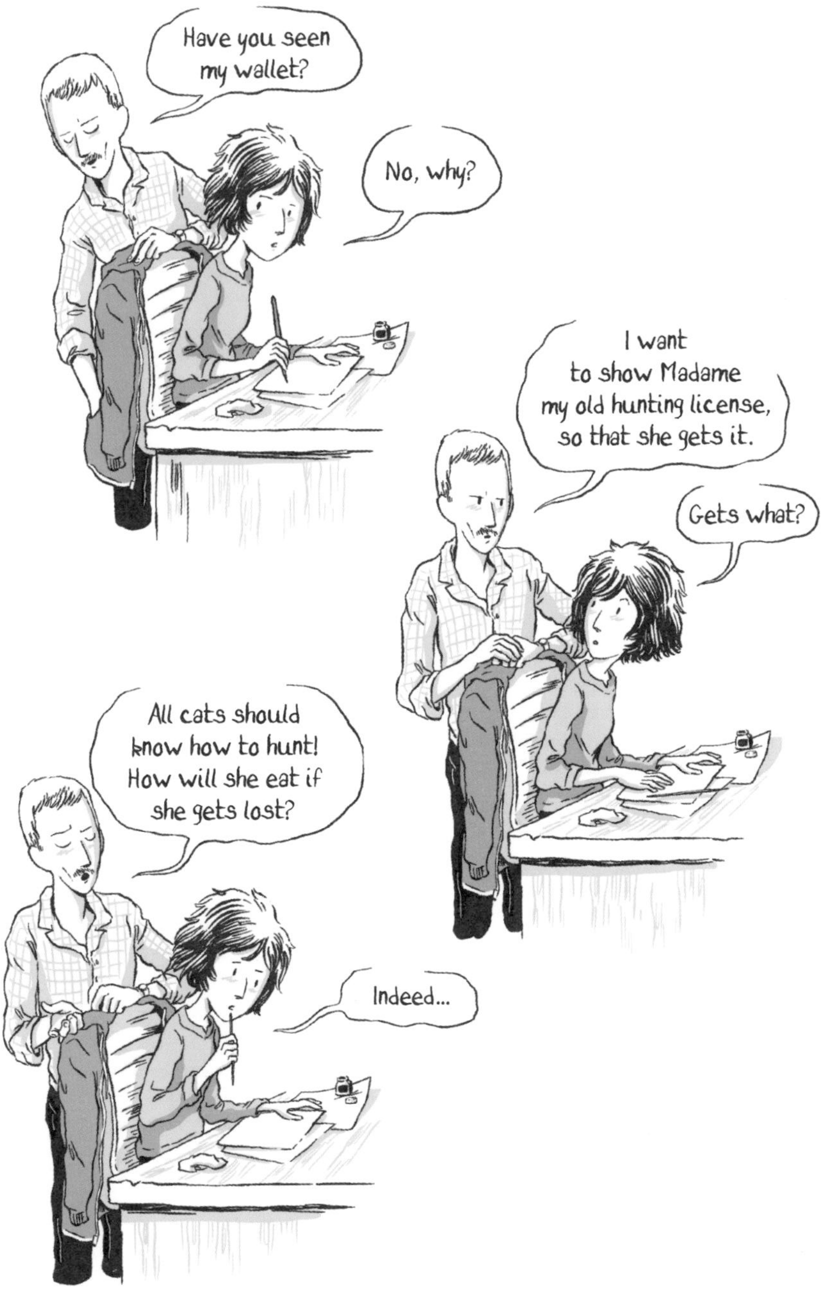
Have you seen my wallet?
No, why?
I want to show Madame my old hunting license, so that she gets it.
Gets what?
All cats should know how to hunt! How will she eat if she gets lost?
Indeed...

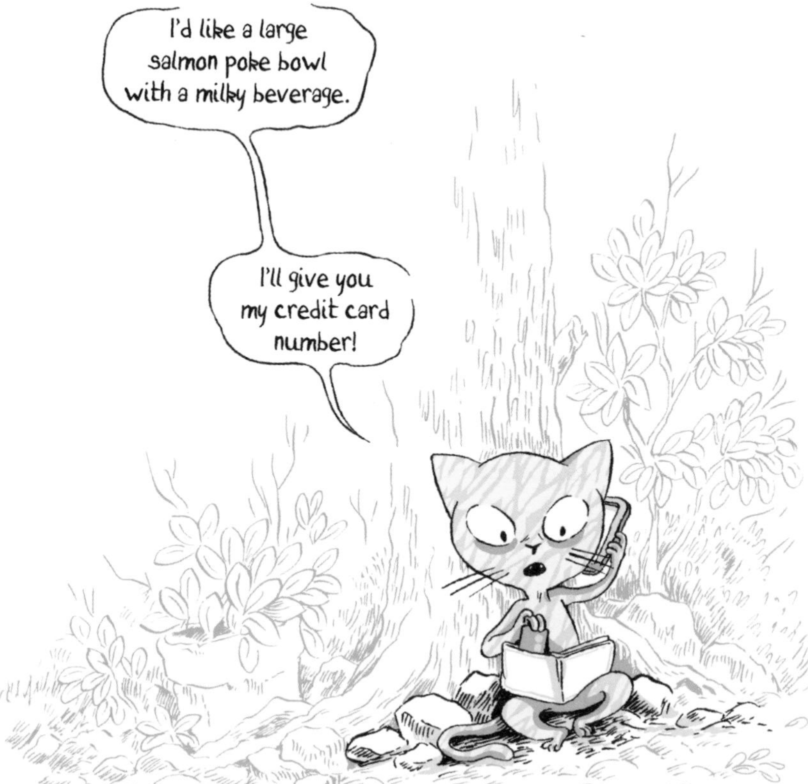
I'd like a large salmon poke bowl with a milky beverage.
I'll give you my credit card number!

Madame overreacts

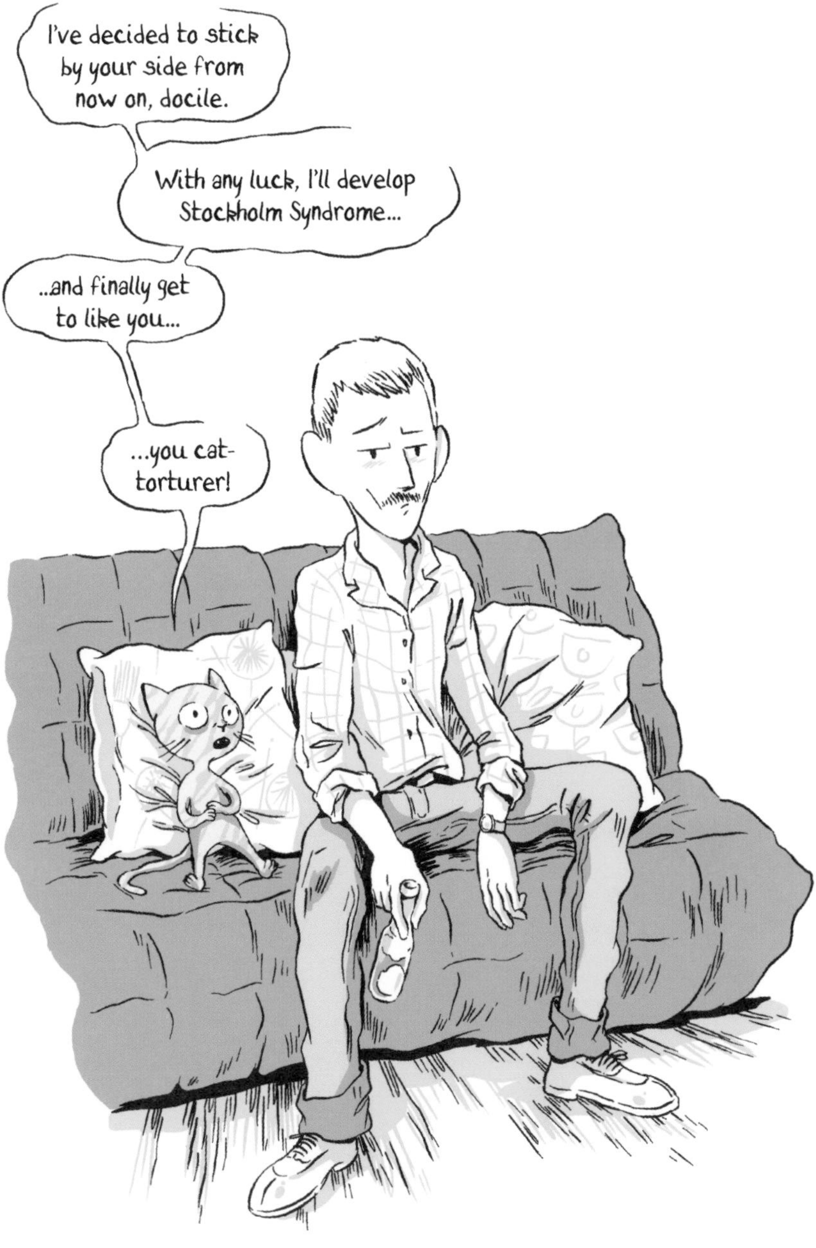
I've decided to stick by your side from now on, docile.
With any luck, I'll develop Stockholm Syndrome...
..and finally get to like you...
...you cat-torturer!

Madame got swag

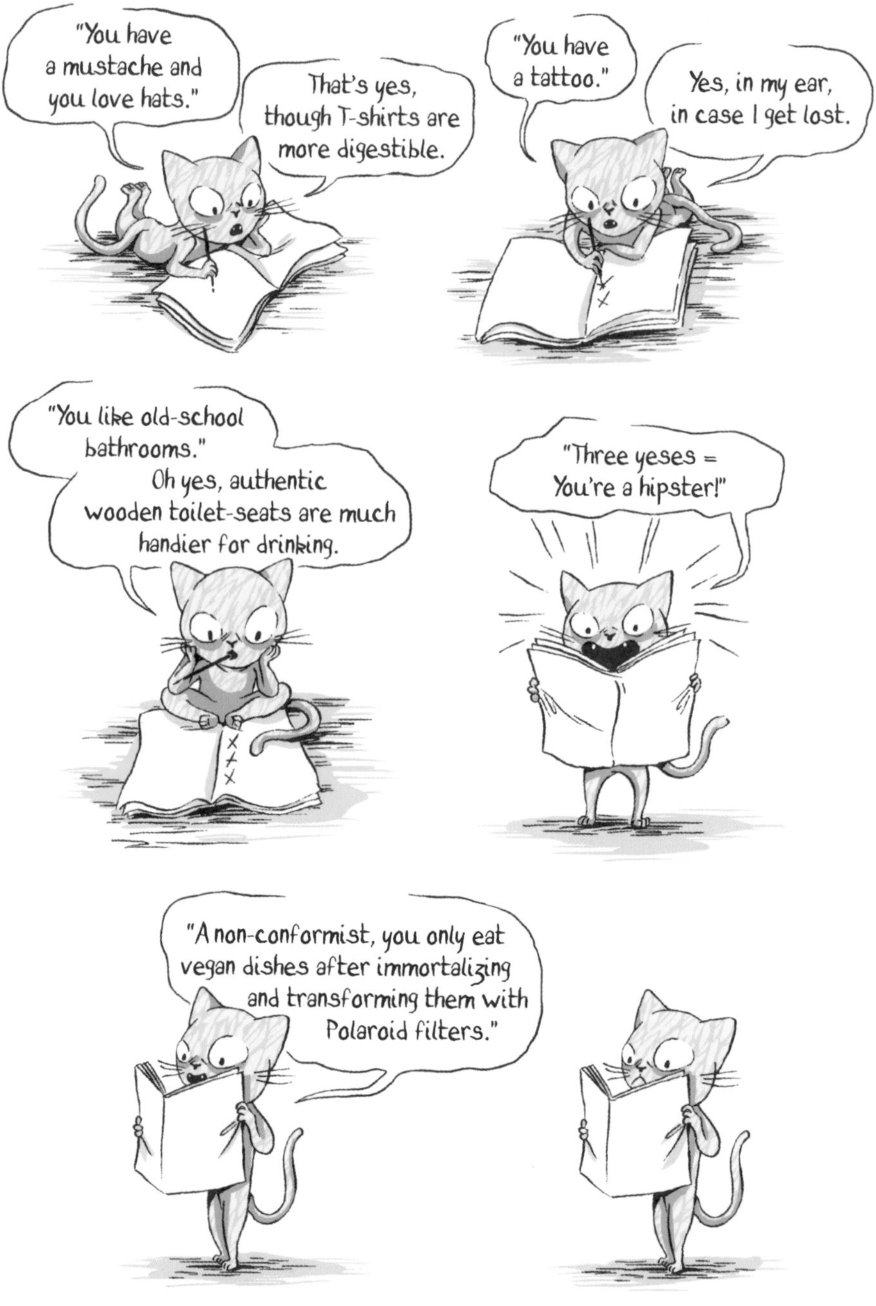
"You have a mustache and you love hats."
That's yes, though T-shirts are more digestible.
"You have a tattoo."
Yes, in my ear, in case I get lost.
"You like old-school bathrooms."
Oh yes, authentic wooden toilet-seats are much handier for drinking.
"Three yeses = You're a hipster!"
"A non-conformist, you only eat vegan dishes after immortalizing and transforming them with Polaroid filters."

What's a Polaroid transformation?
Can it turn vegetables into meat?
No.

It turns vegetables into vintage veggies.

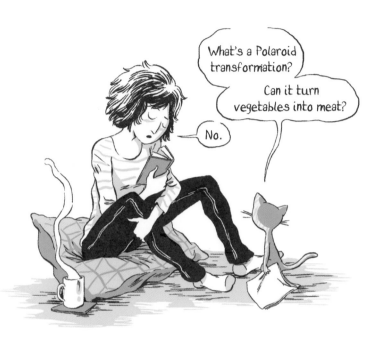

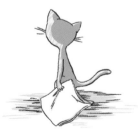

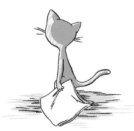

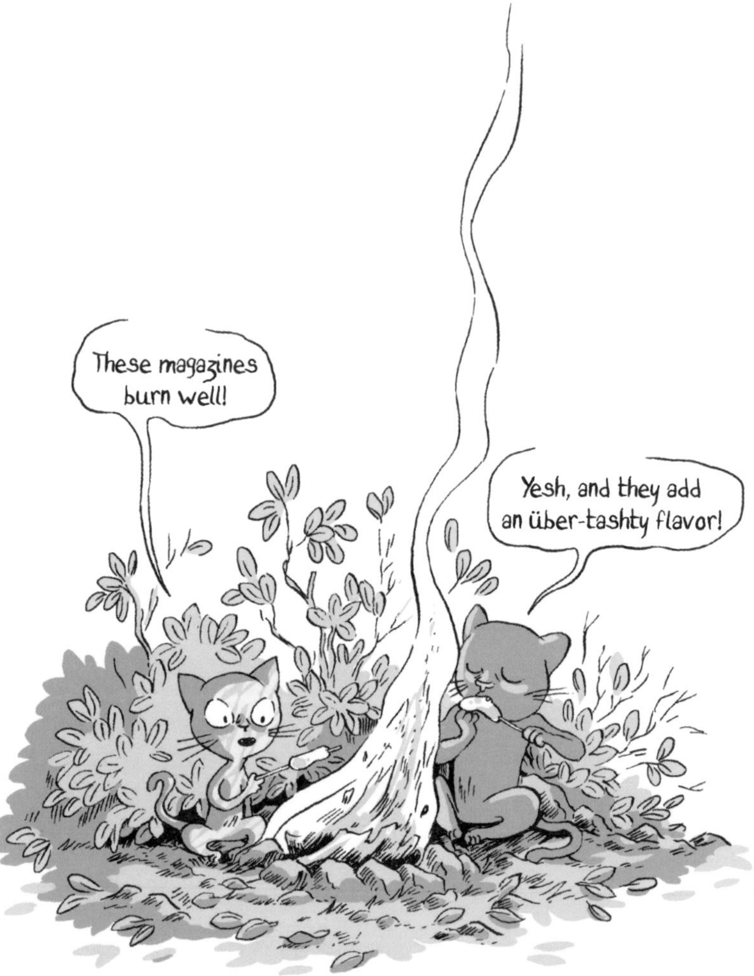
These magazines burn well!
Yesh, and they add an über-tashty flavor!

Madame scours

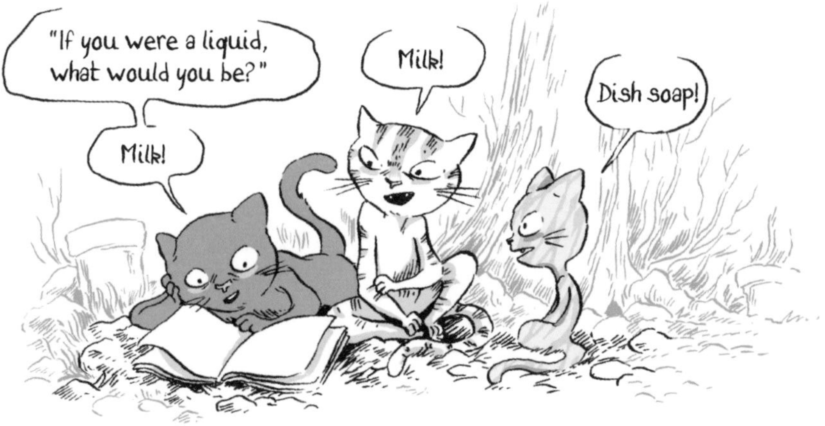
"If you were a liquid, what would you be?"
Milk!
Milk!
Dish soap!

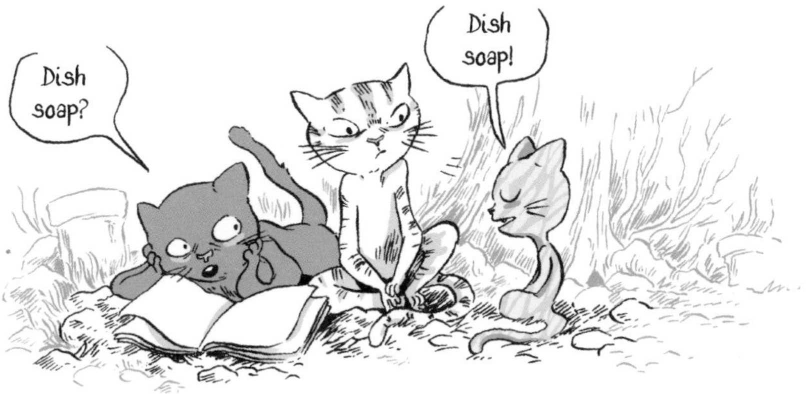
Dish soap?
Dish soap!

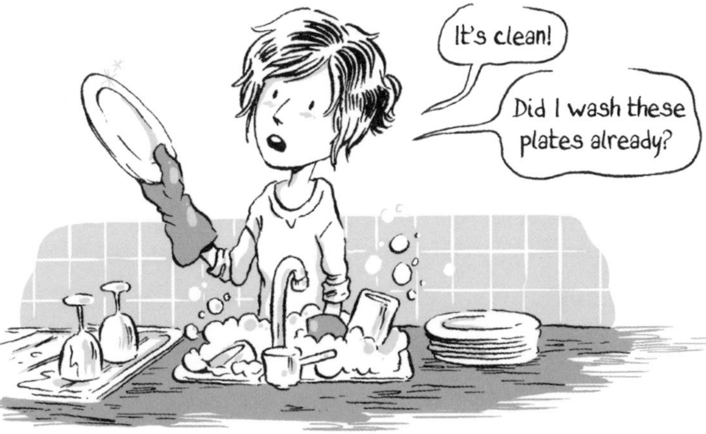
It's clean!
Did I wash these plates already?

Madame deterges

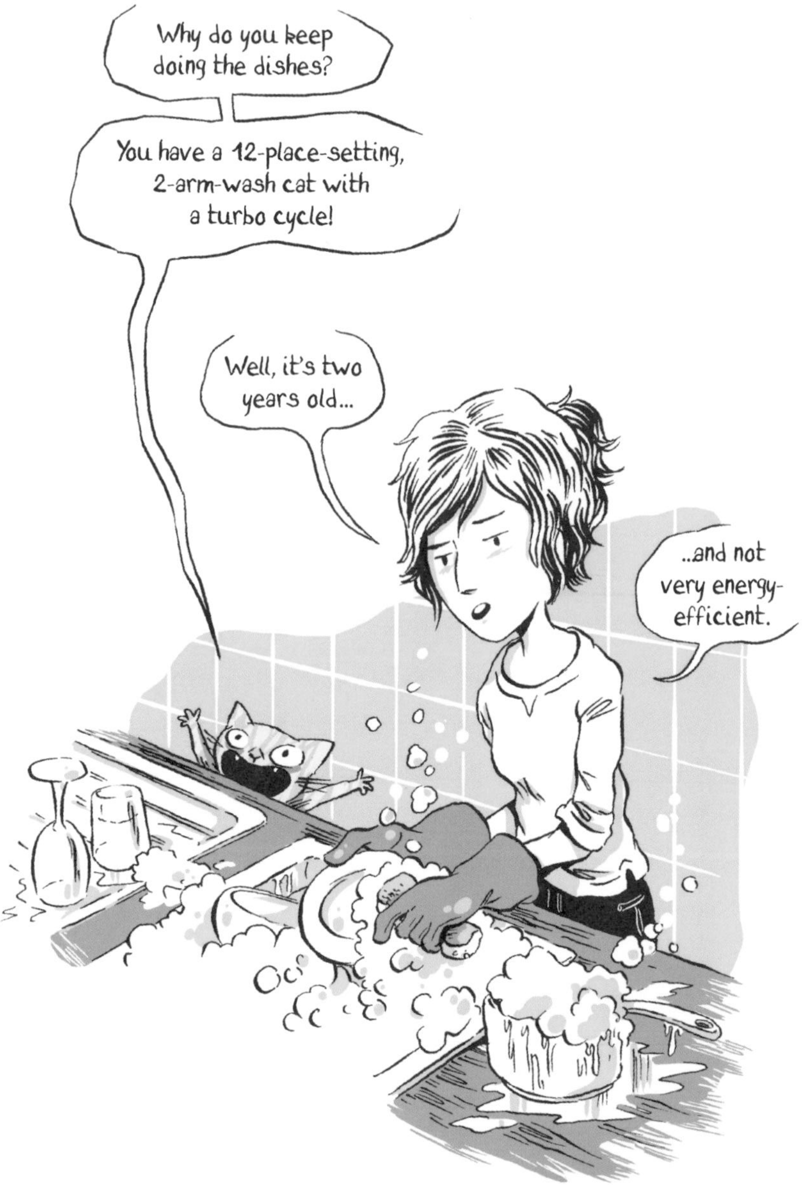
Why do you keep doing the dishes?
You have a 12-place-setting, 2-arm-wash cat with a turbo cycle!
Well, it's two years old...
..and not very energy-efficient.

Madame wraps

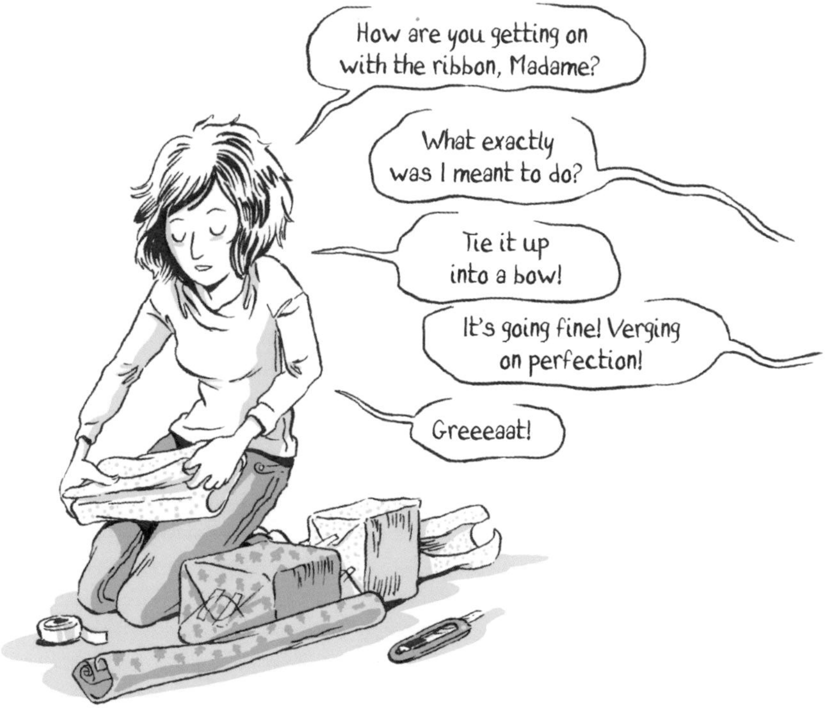
How are you getting on with the ribbon, Madame?
What exactly was I meant to do?
Tie it up into a bow!
It's going fine! Verging on perfection!
Greeeaat!

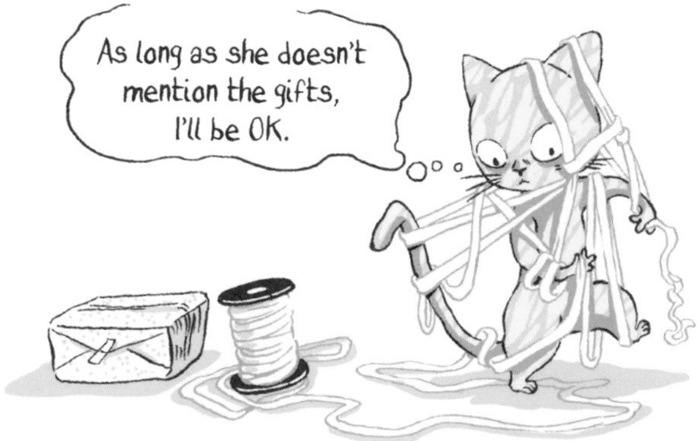
As long as she doesn't mention the gifts, I'll be OK.

Madame parcels

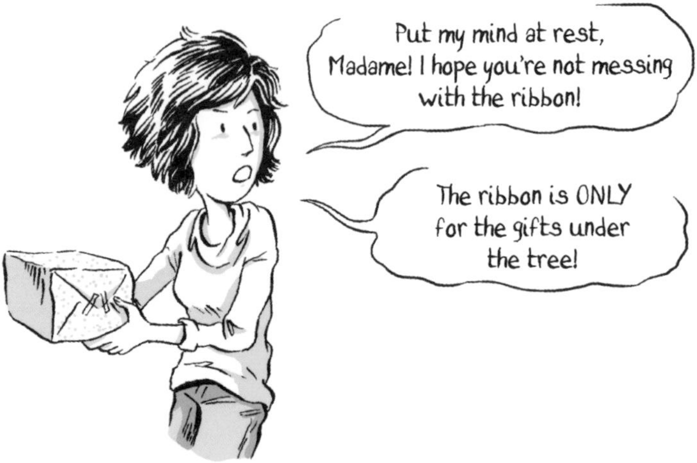
Put my mind at rest, Madame! I hope you're not messing with the ribbon!
The ribbon is ONLY for the gifts under the tree!

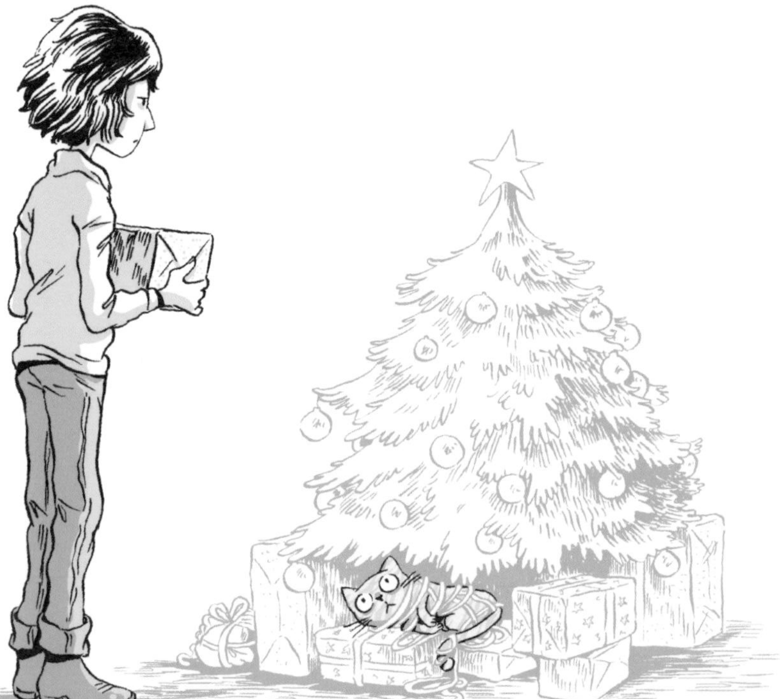

Madame dreams

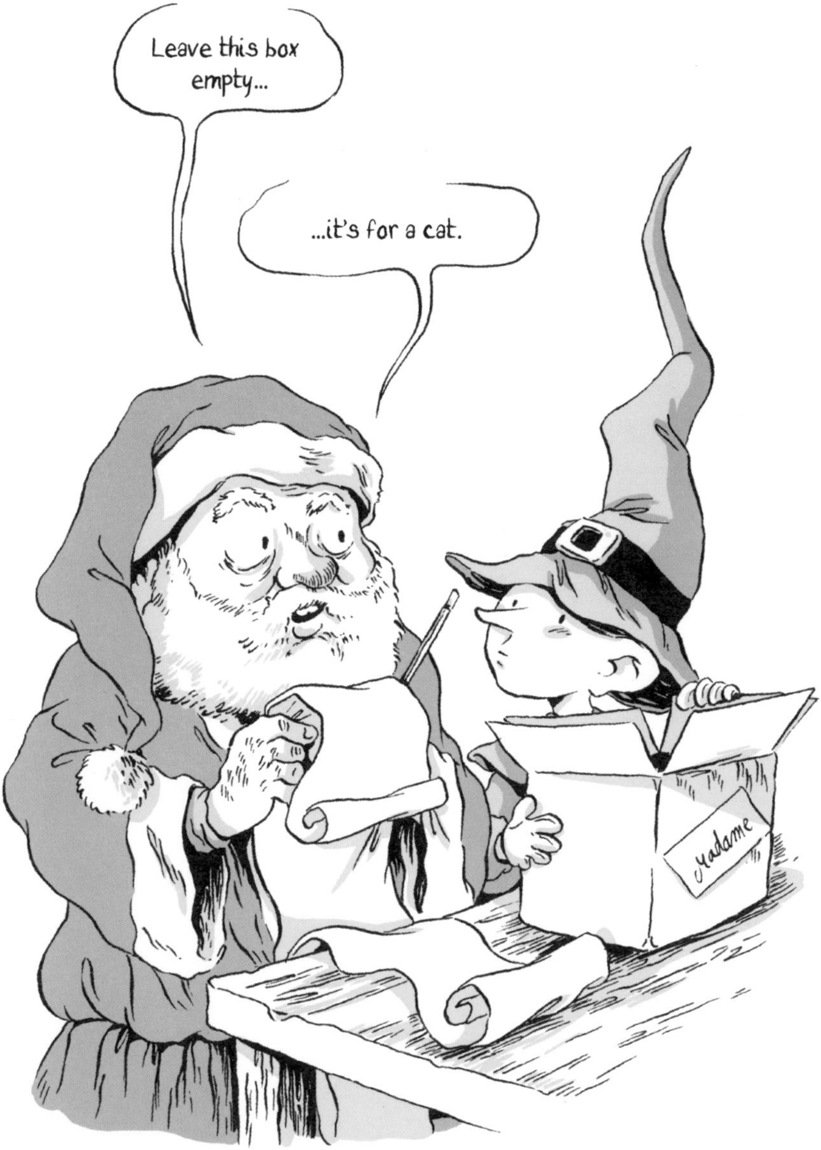
Leave this box empty...
...it's for a cat.
Madame

Madame baits

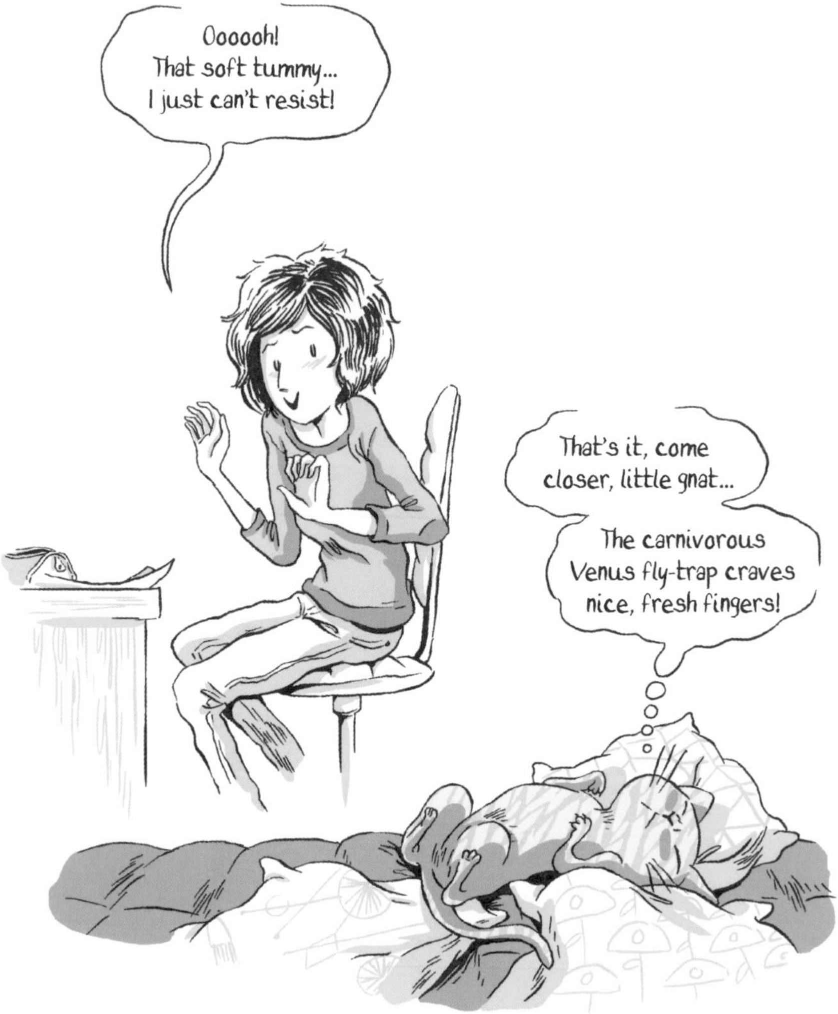
Oooooh!
That soft tummy...
I just can't resist!
That's it, come closer, little gnat...
The carnivorous Venus fly-trap craves nice, fresh fingers!

Madame treks

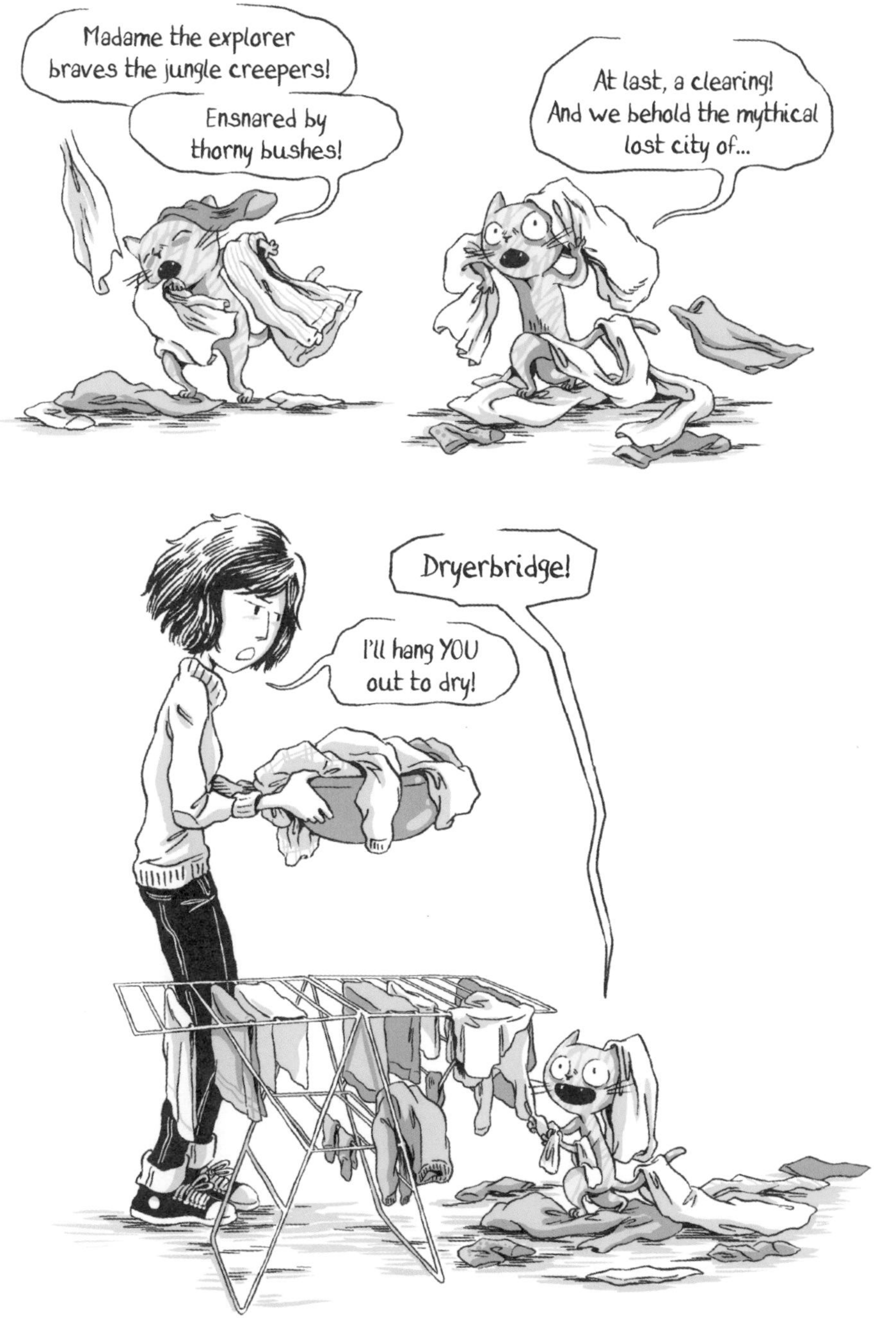

Madame the explorer braves the jungle creepers!
Ensnared by thorny bushes!
At last, a clearing! And we behold the mythical lost city of...
Dryerbridge!
I'll hang YOU out to dry!

Madame spells

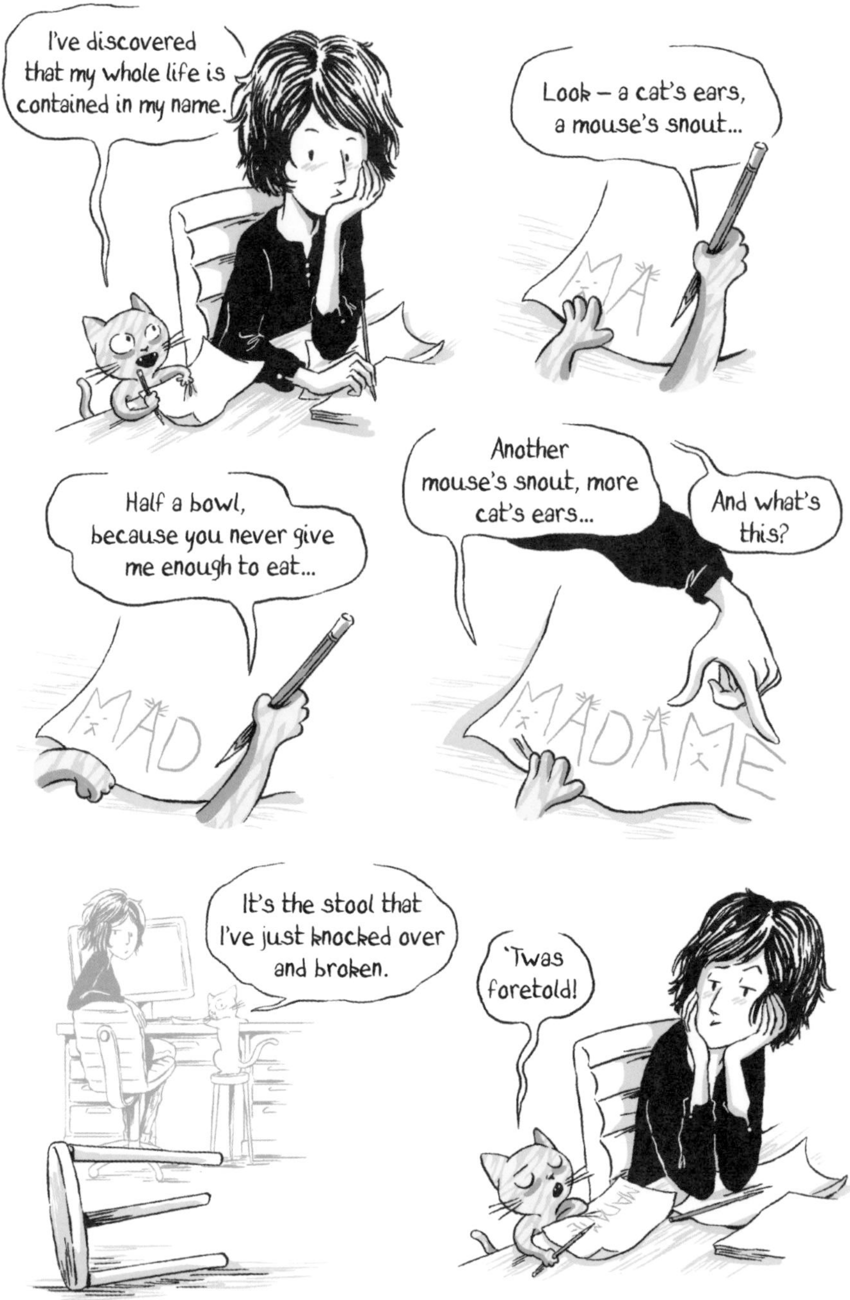
I've discovered that my whole life is contained in my name.
Look – a cat's ears, a mouse's snout...
MA
Half a bowl, because you never give me enough to eat...
MAD
Another mouse's snout, more cat's ears...
And what's this?
MADAME
It's the stool that I've just knocked over and broken.
'Twas foretold!

Madame decompresses

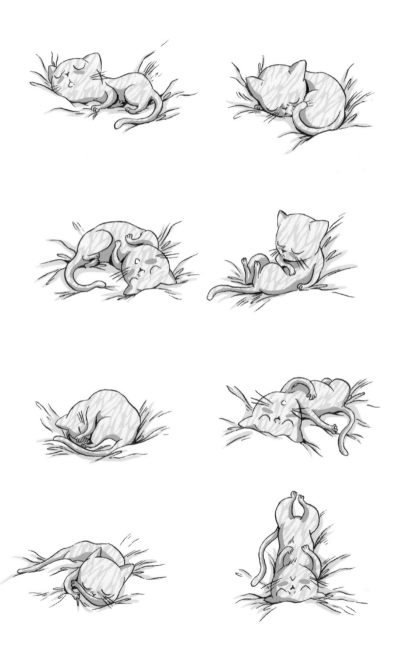

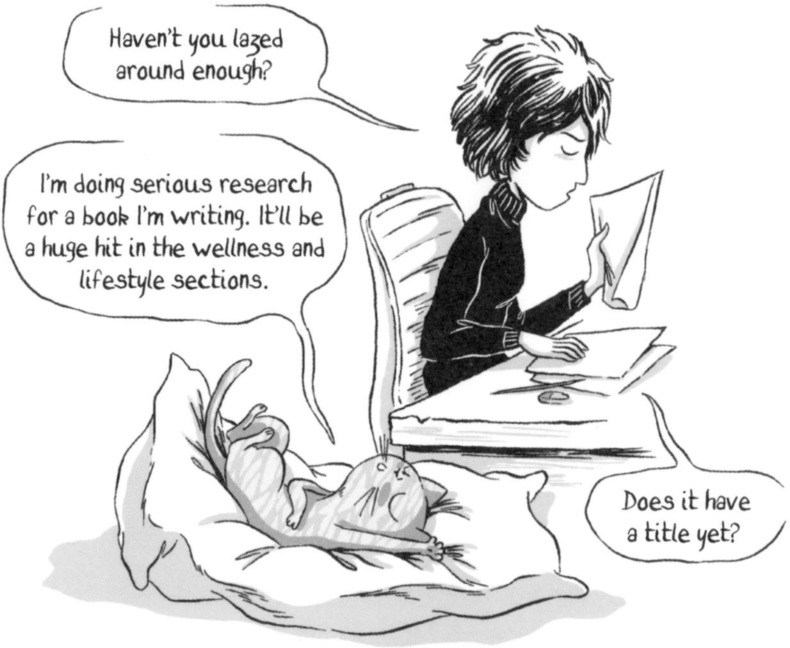
Haven't you lazed around enough?
I'm doing serious research for a book I'm writing. It'll be a huge hit in the wellness and lifestyle sections.
Does it have a title yet?

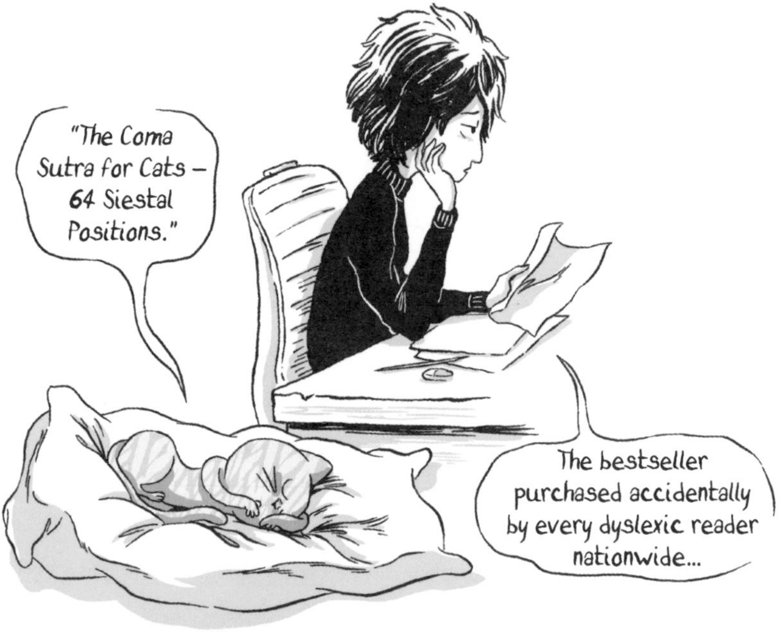
"The Coma Sutra for Cats – 64 Siestal Positions."
The bestseller purchased accidentally by every dyslexic reader nationwide...

Madame authors

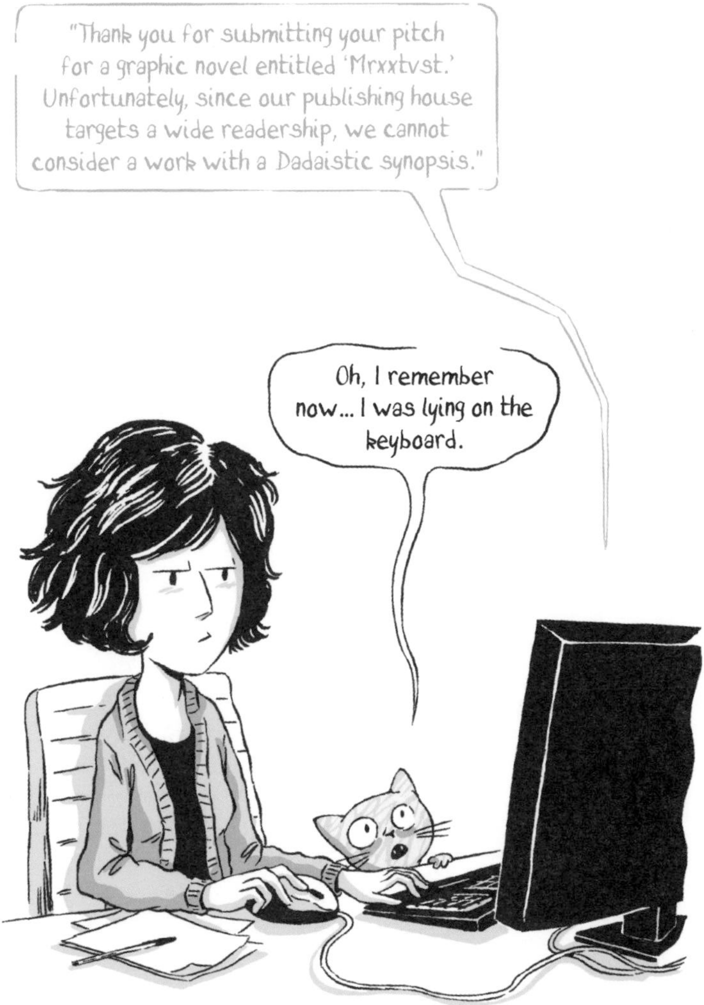
"Thank you for submitting your pitch for a graphic novel entitled 'Mrxxtvst.' Unfortunately, since our publishing house targets a wide readership, we cannot consider a work with a Dadaistic synopsis."
Oh, I remember now... I was lying on the keyboard.

Madame demands

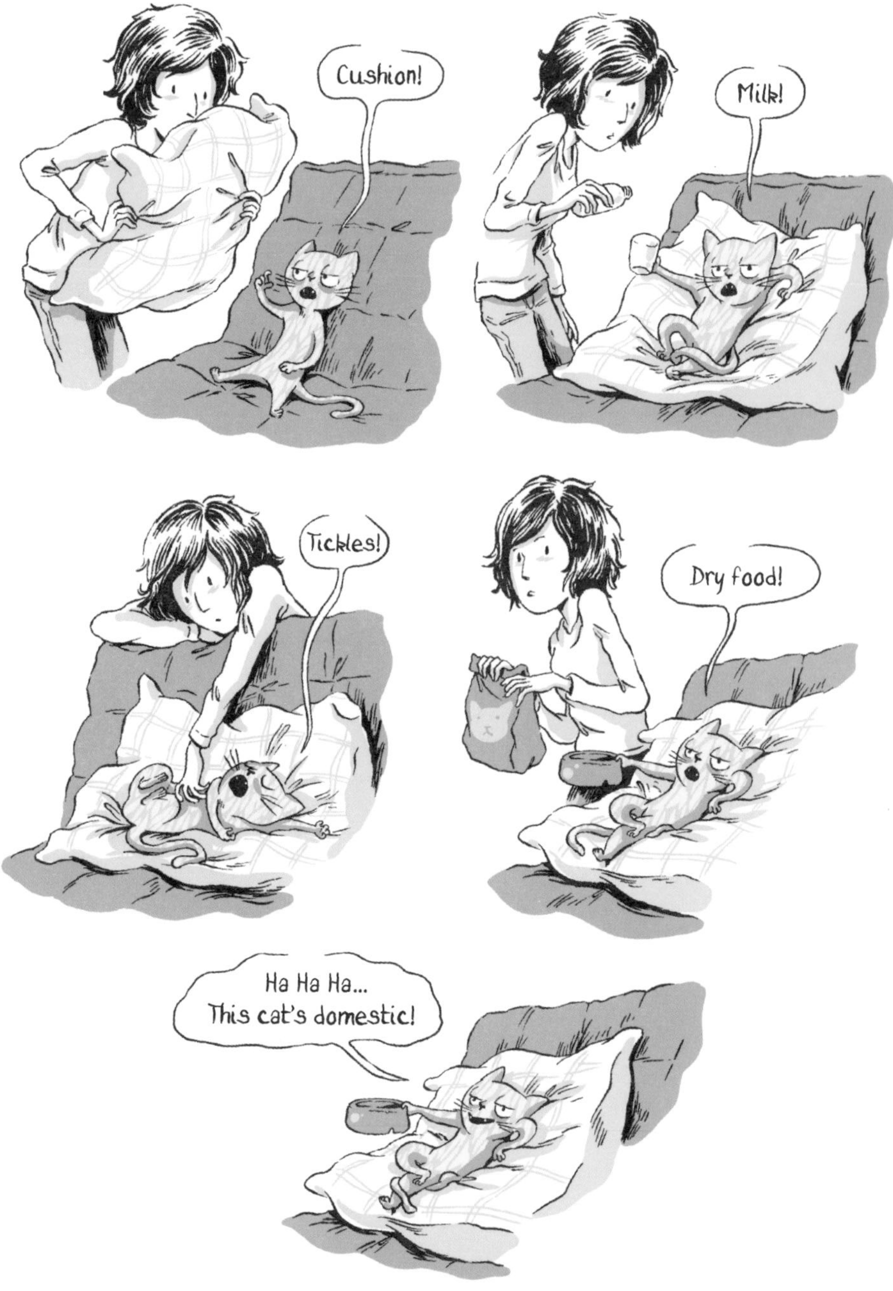
Cushion!
Milk!
Tickles!
Dry food!
Ha Ha Ha...
This cat's domestic!

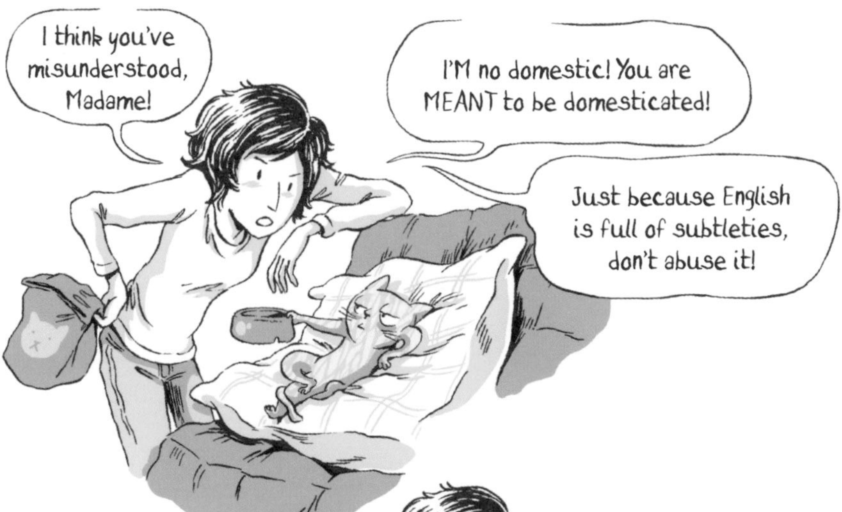
I think you've misunderstood, Madame!
I'M no domestic! You are MEANT to be domesticated!
Just because English is full of subtleties, don't abuse it!

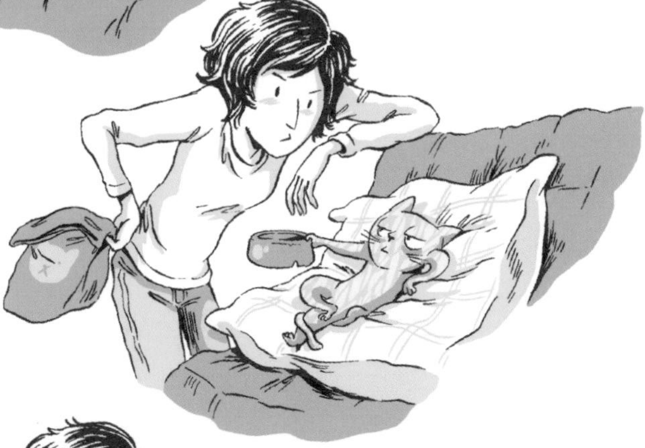

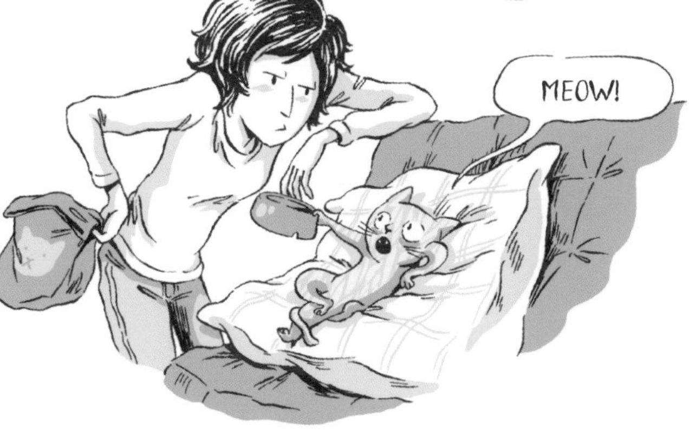
MEOW!

BEER!

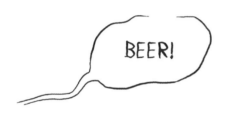

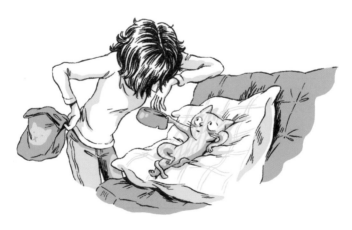

Madame terminates

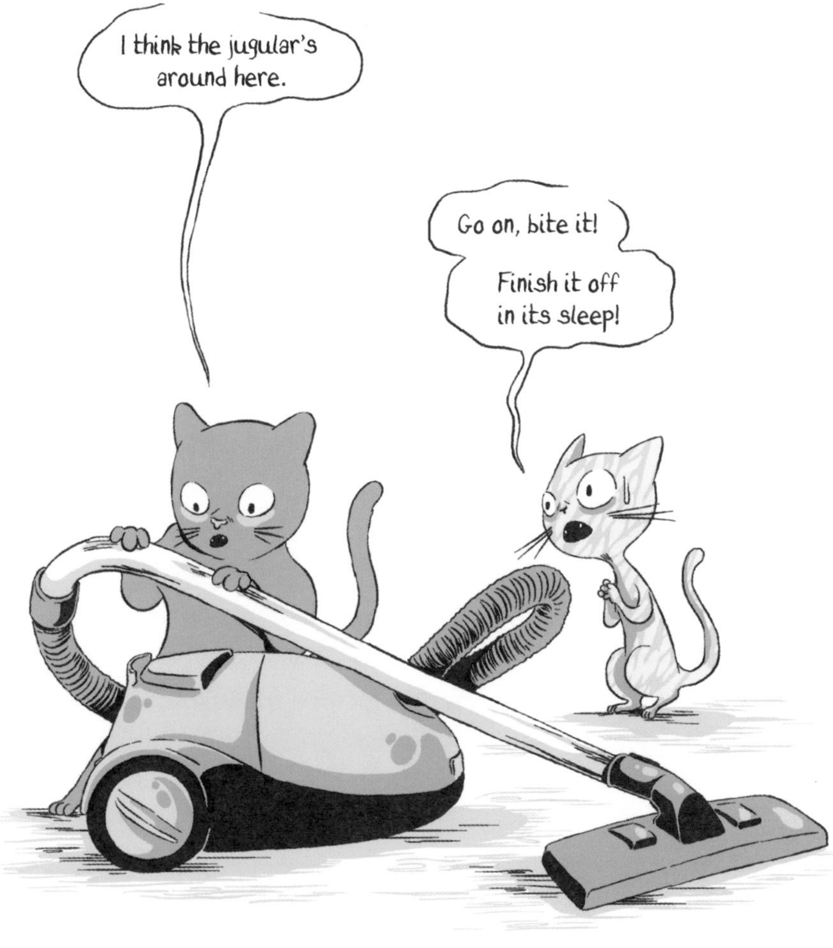
I think the jugular's around here.
Go on, bite it!
Finish it off in its sleep!

Madame tires

Body language: the beached seal position.

"You're going to the bakery
and leaving me all alone."

"I'm dehydrated and I need milk."

"I'm bored out of my mind, but you
don't have time to play with me."

"At 7 pm, he'll get back from work,
and you'll forget I exist."

"This cat wears me out."

Madame applies

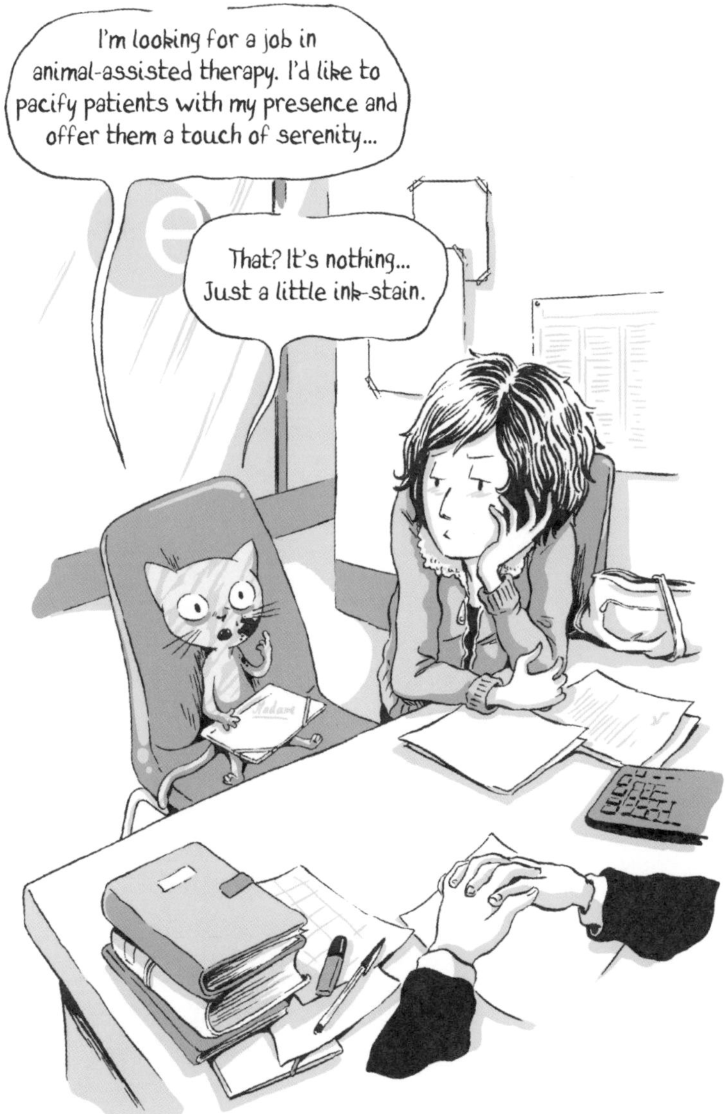
I'm looking for a job in animal-assisted therapy. I'd like to pacify patients with my presence and offer them a touch of serenity...
That? It's nothing... Just a little ink-stain.
Madame

Madame reapplies

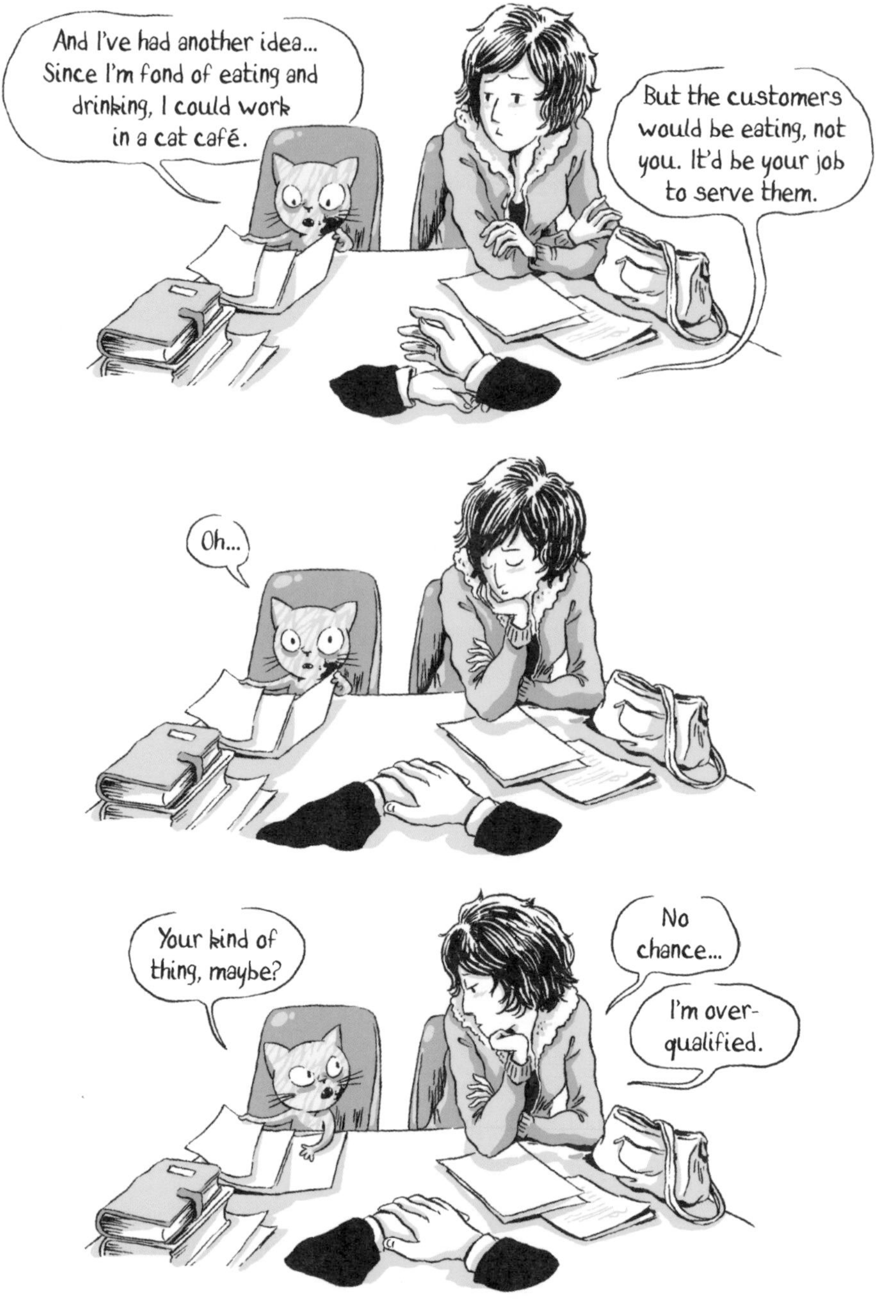
And I've had another idea... Since I'm fond of eating and drinking, I could work in a cat café.
But the customers would be eating, not you. It'd be your job to serve them.
Oh...
Your kind of thing, maybe?
No chance...
I'm over-qualified.

Madame researches

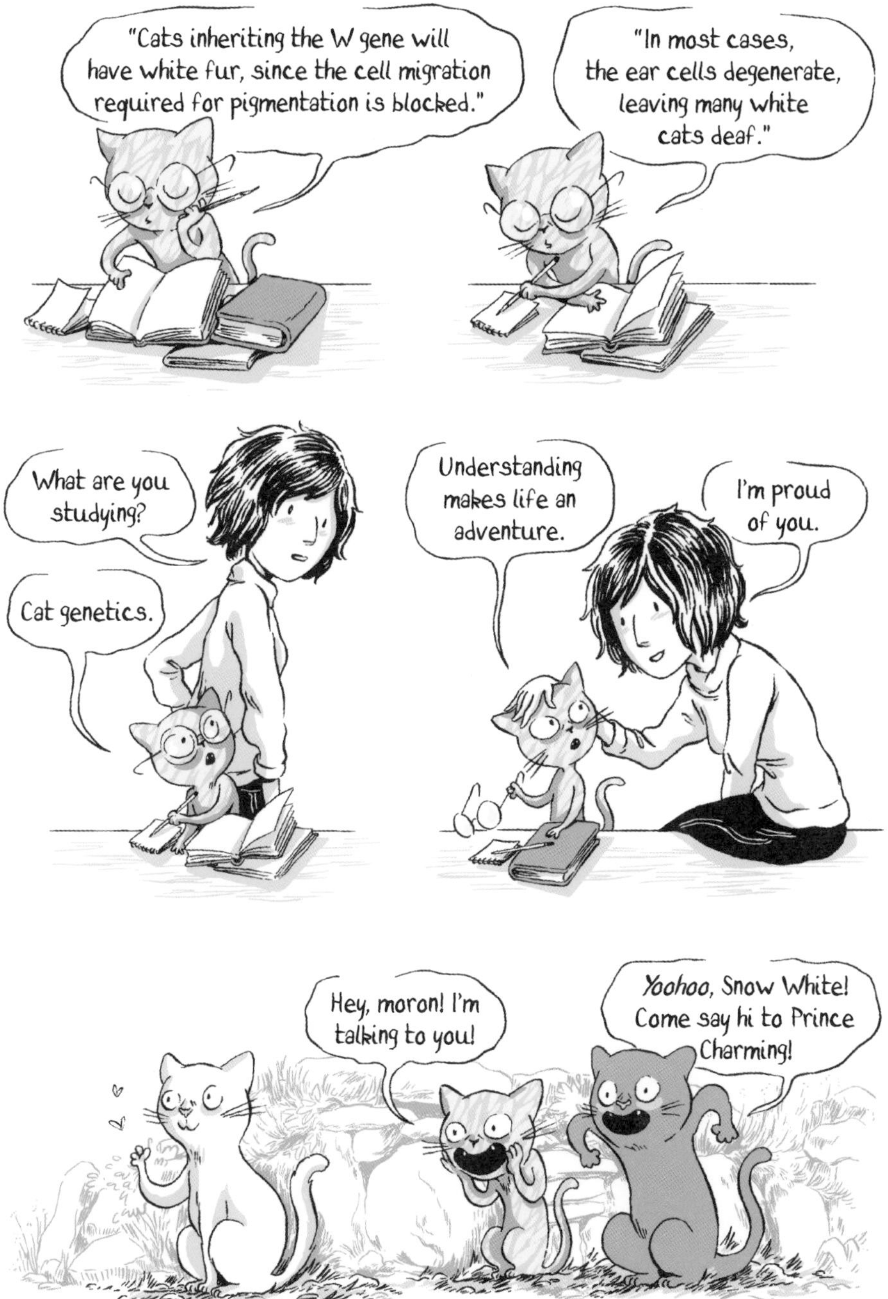
"Cats inheriting the W gene will have white fur, since the cell migration required for pigmentation is blocked."
"In most cases, the ear cells degenerate, leaving many white cats deaf."
What are you studying?
Cat genetics.
Understanding makes life an adventure.
I'm proud of you.
Hey, moron! I'm talking to you!
Yoohoo, Snow White! Come say hi to Prince Charming!

Madame reaps

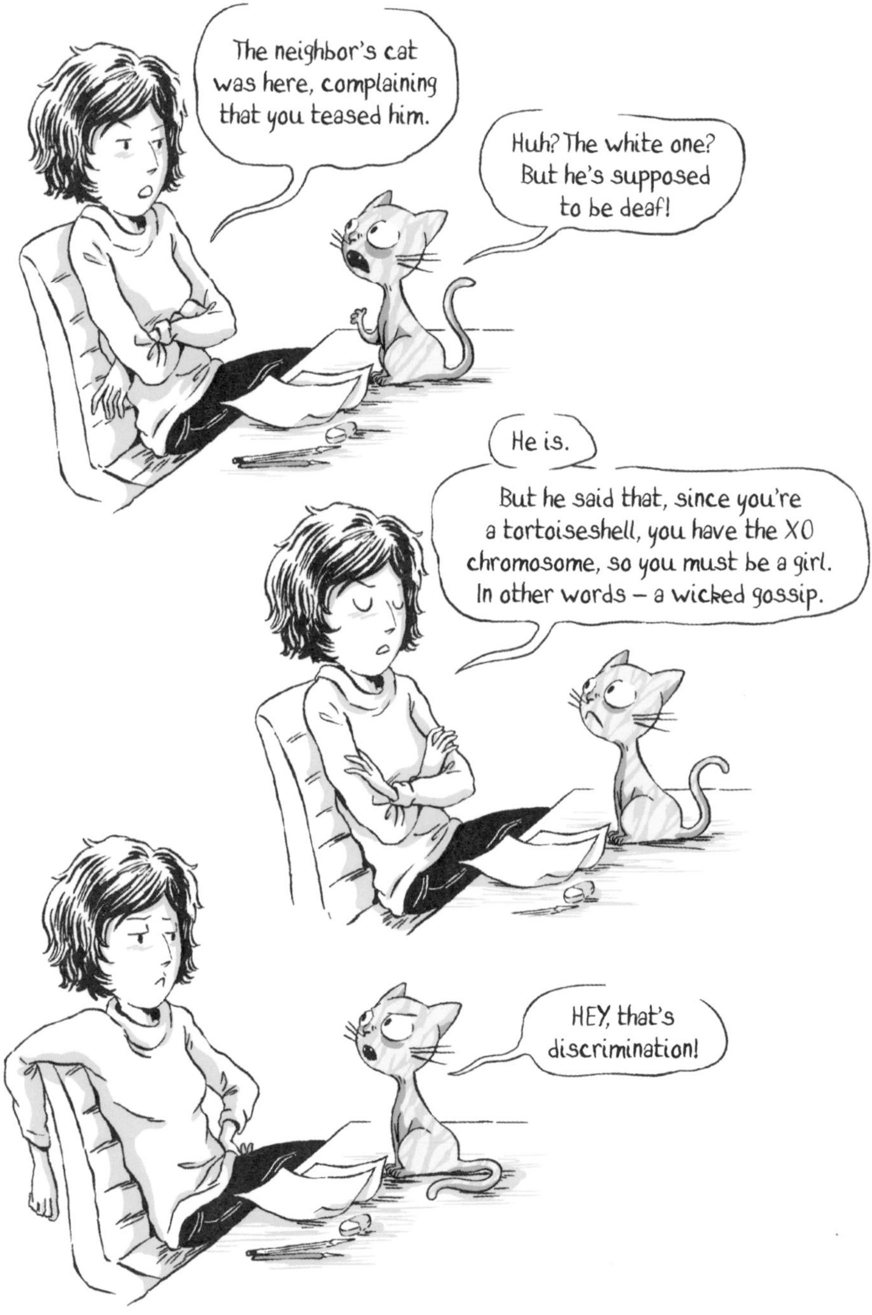
The neighbor's cat was here, complaining that you teased him.
Huh? The white one? But he's supposed to be deaf!
He is.
But he said that, since you're a tortoiseshell, you have the XO chromosome, so you must be a girl. In other words – a wicked gossip.
HEY, that's discrimination!

Madame smashes

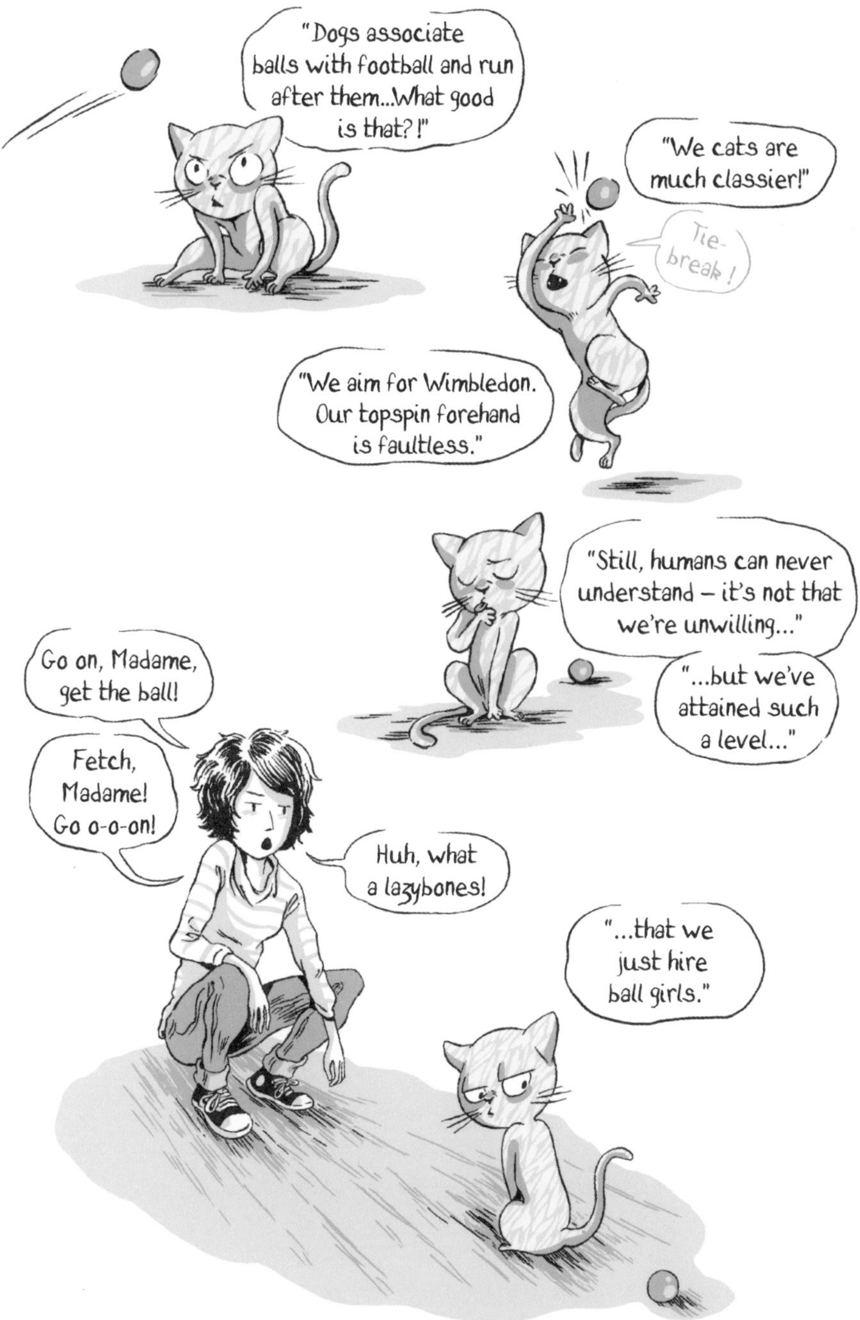
"Dogs associate balls with football and run after them...What good is that?!"
"We cats are much classier!"
Tie-break!
"We aim for Wimbledon. Our topspin forehand is faultless."
"Still, humans can never understand – it's not that we're unwilling..."
"...but we've attained such a level..."
Go on, Madame, get the ball!
Fetch, Madame! Go o-o-on!
Huh, what a lazybones!
"...that we just hire ball girls."

Madame blares

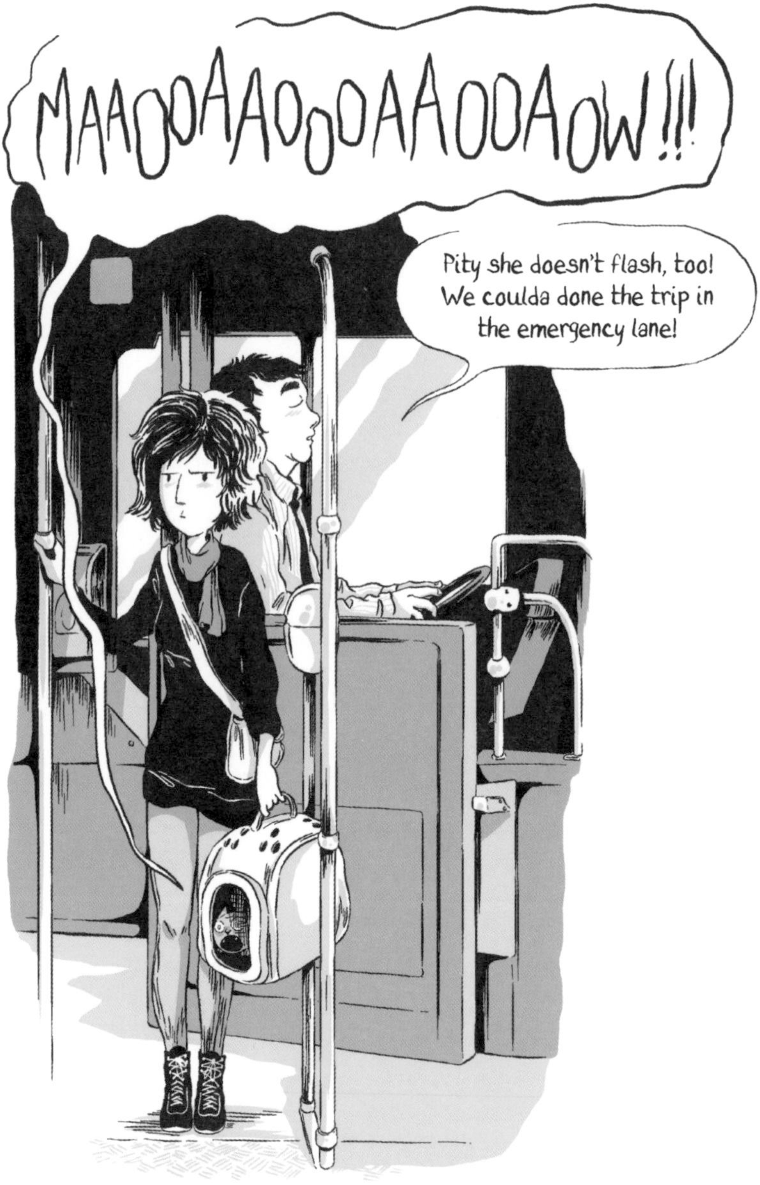
MAAOOAAOOOOAAOOAOW!!!
Pity she doesn't flash, too! We coulda done the trip in the emergency lane!

Madame diagnoses

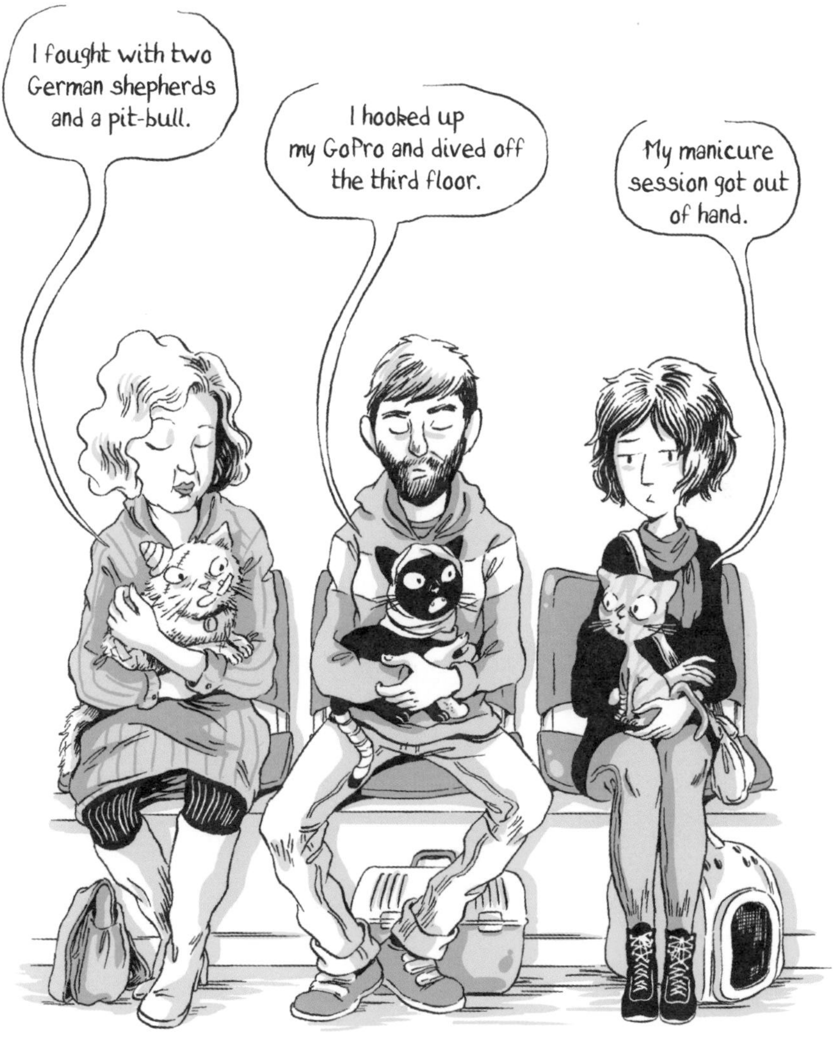
I fought with two German shepherds and a pit-bull.
I hooked up my GoPro and dived off the third floor.
My manicure session got out of hand.

Madame facelifts

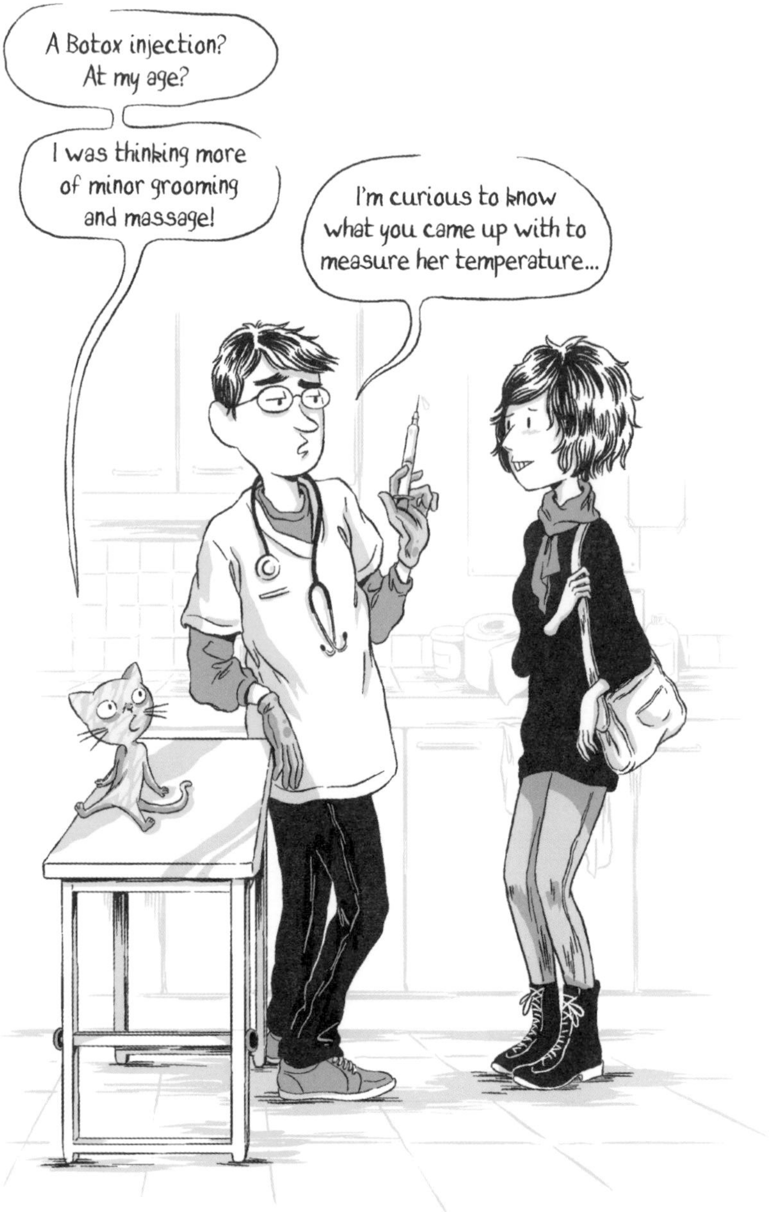
A Botox injection? At my age?
I was thinking more of minor grooming and massage!
I'm curious to know what you came up with to measure her temperature...

Madame sneaks a peek

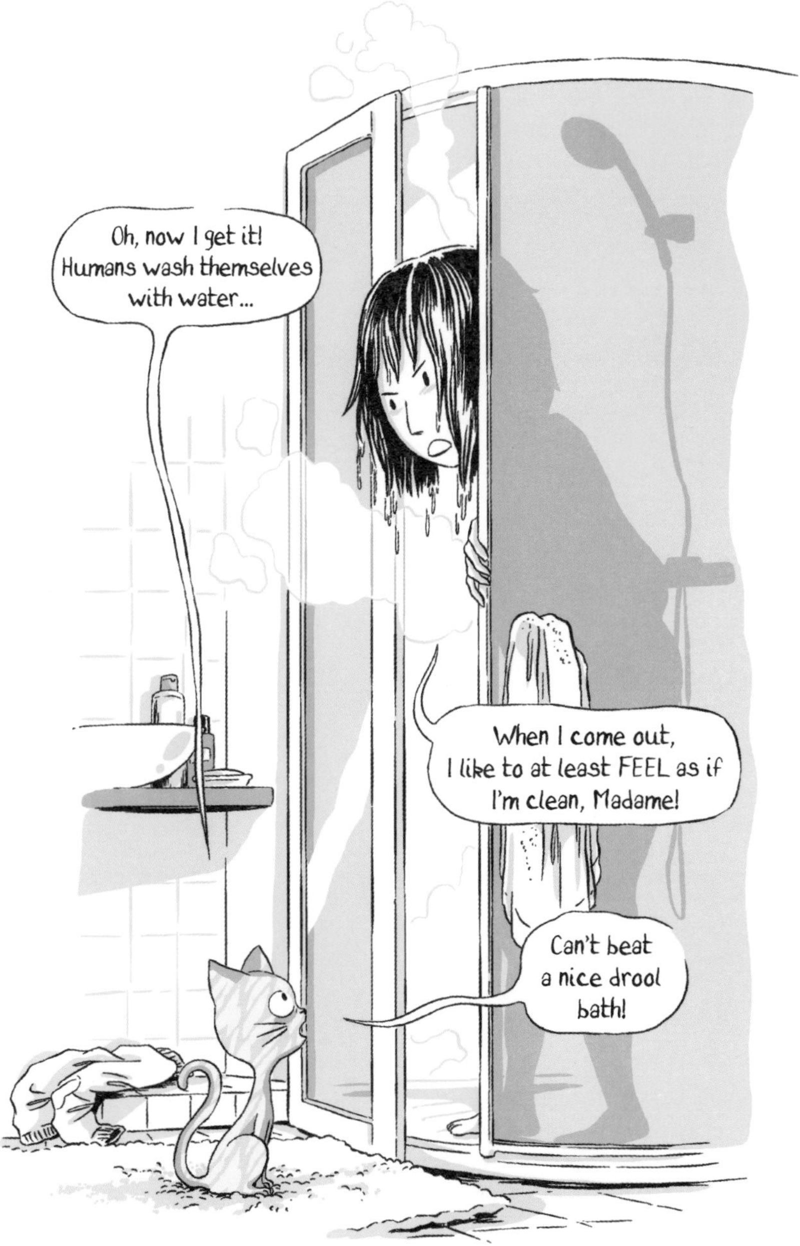
Oh, now I get it! Humans wash themselves with water...
When I come out, I like to at least FEEL as if I'm clean, Madame!
Can't beat a nice drool bath!

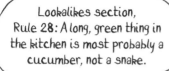

Lookalikes section, Rule 28: A long, green thing in the kitchen is most probably a cucumber, not a snake.

Rule 29: Tone of voice doesn't always convey the actual meaning. For instance, "Nasty, nasty kitty!" is not a compliment.

Rule 30: A decorated, flat, rectangular surface isn't always a fancy mattress.

It's true, you were right. I DID note that one down in my book!

Madame wakes

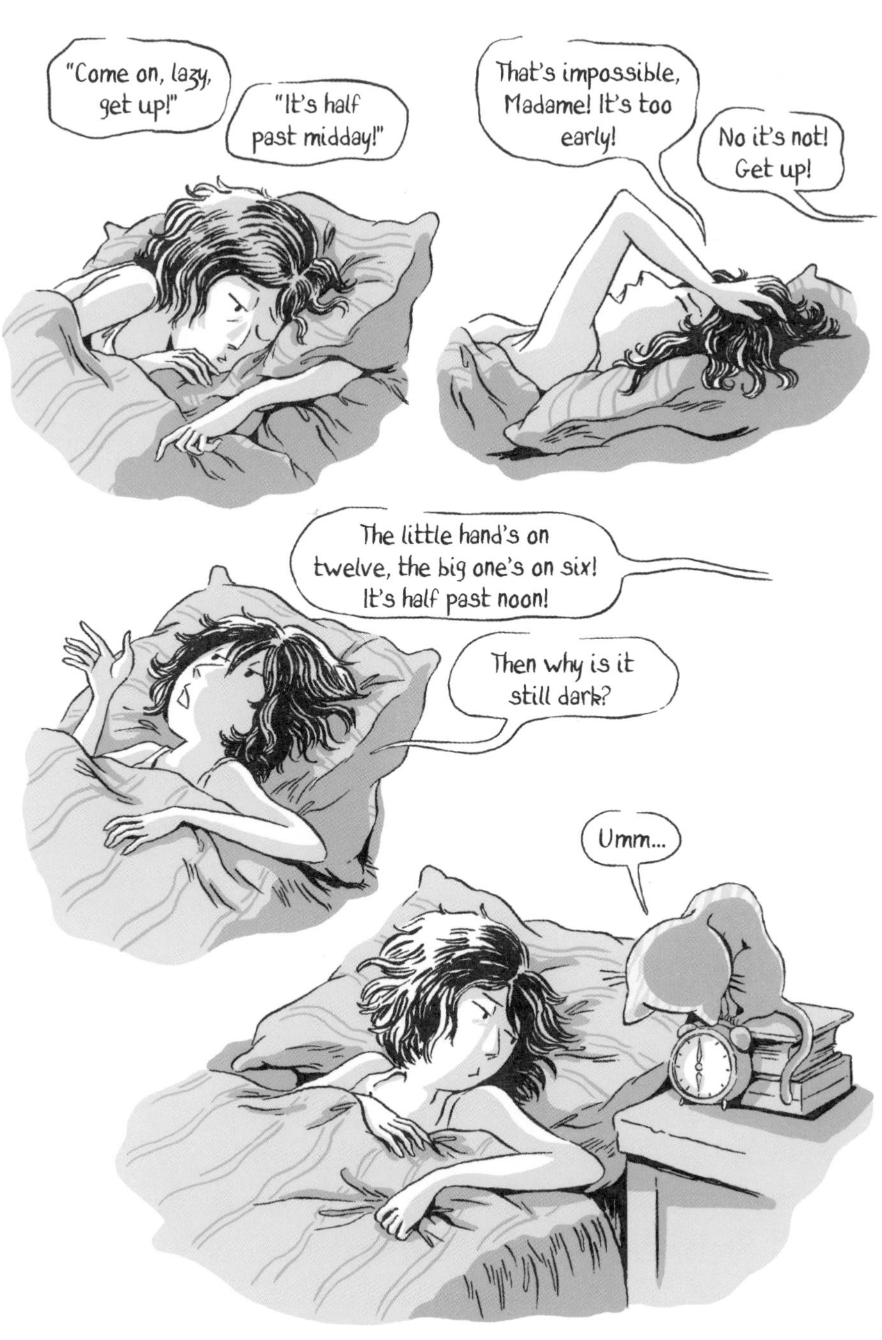
"Come on, lazy, get up!"
"It's half past midday!"
That's impossible, Madame! It's too early!
No it's not! Get up!
The little hand's on twelve, the big one's on six! It's half past noon!
Then why is it still dark?
Umm...

Madame caterwauls

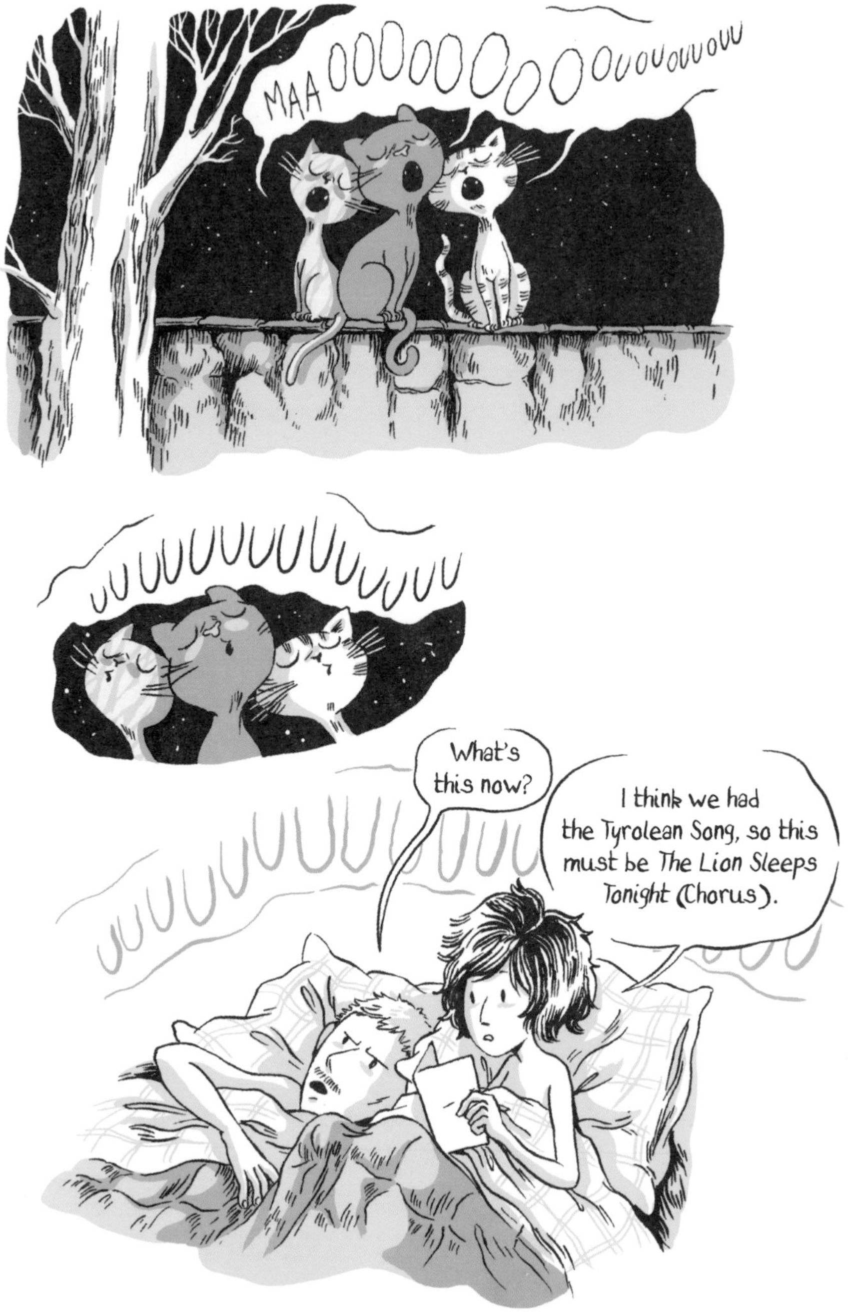
MAA OOOOOOOOOOOuuouuuouu
UUUUUUUUUUUUUUU
What's this now?
I think we had the Tyrolean Song, so this must be *The Lion Sleeps Tonight* (Chorus).

Madame sympathizes

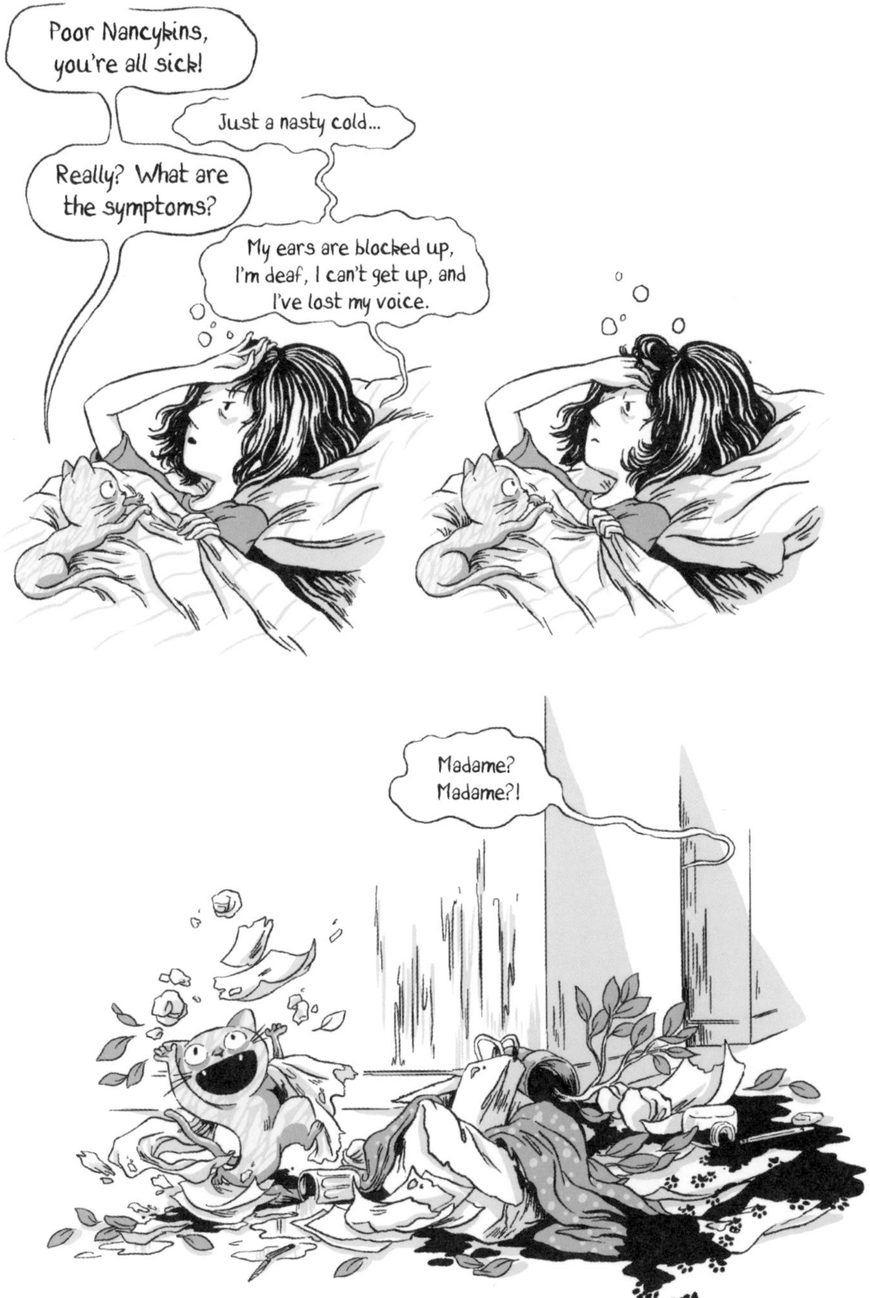
Poor Nancykins, you're all sick!
Just a nasty cold...
Really? What are the symptoms?
My ears are blocked up, I'm deaf, I can't get up, and I've lost my voice.
Madame? Madame?!

Madame scrolls
How to sleep in retro-gaming mode:

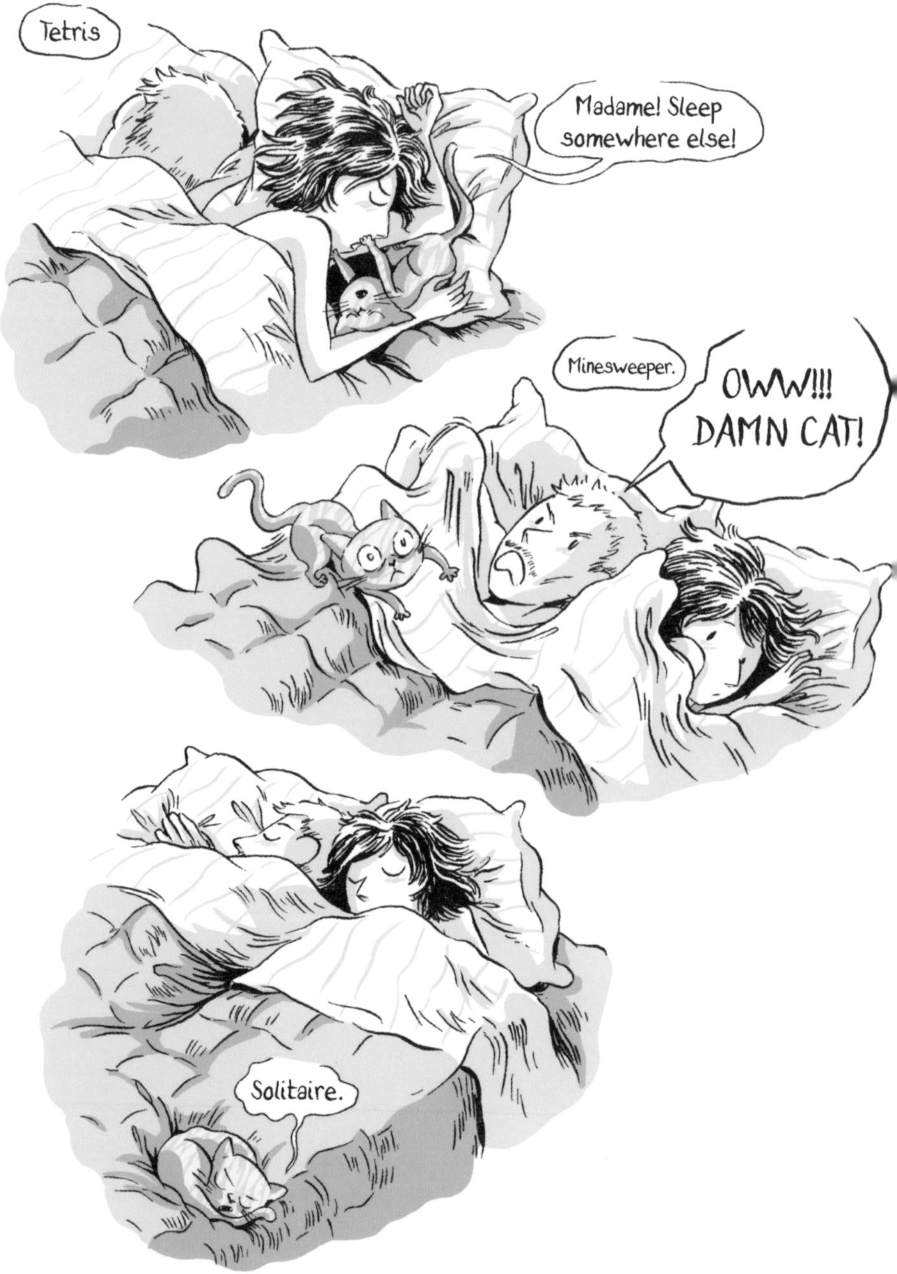
Tetris
Madame! Sleep somewhere else!
Minesweeper.
OWW!!! DAMN CAT!
Solitaire.

Madame savors

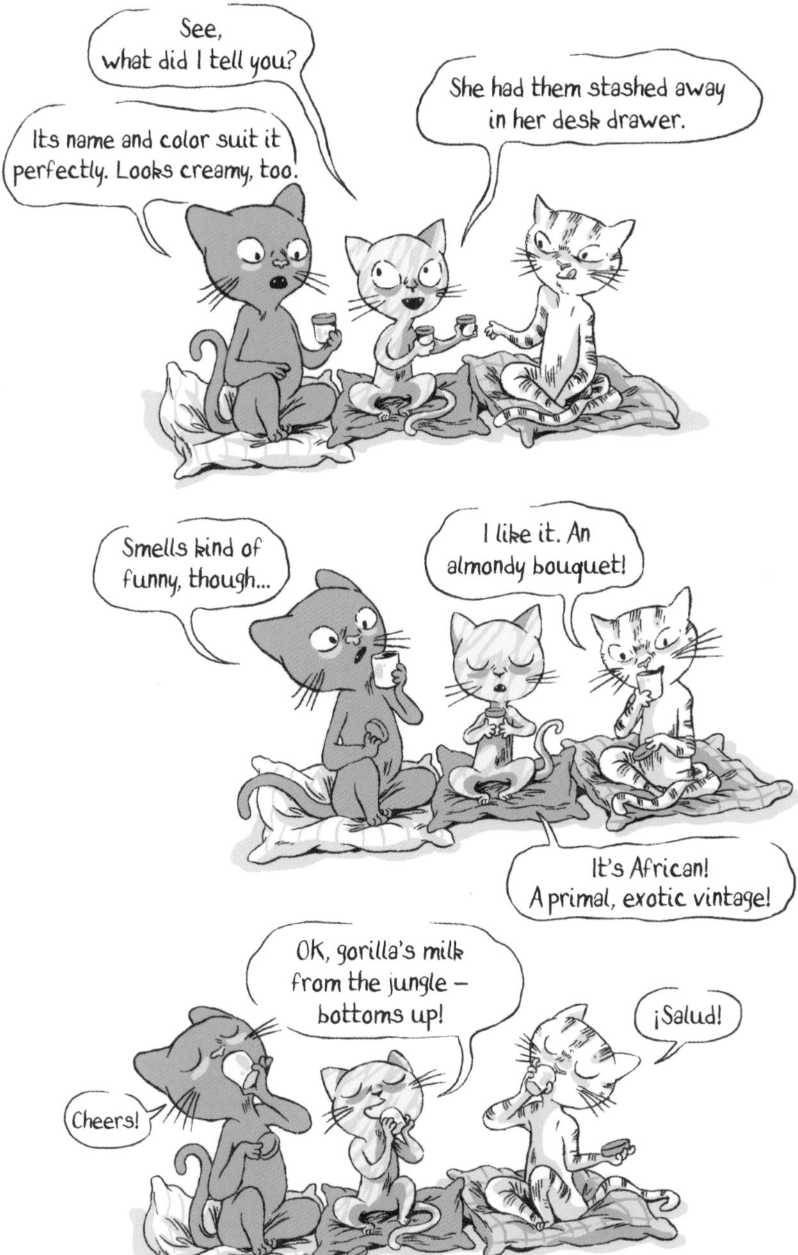

See, what did I tell you?
Its name and color suit it perfectly. Looks creamy, too.
She had them stashed away in her desk drawer.
Smells kind of funny, though...
I like it. An almondy bouquet!
It's African! A primal, exotic vintage!
OK, gorilla's milk from the jungle – bottoms up!
¡Salud!
Cheers!

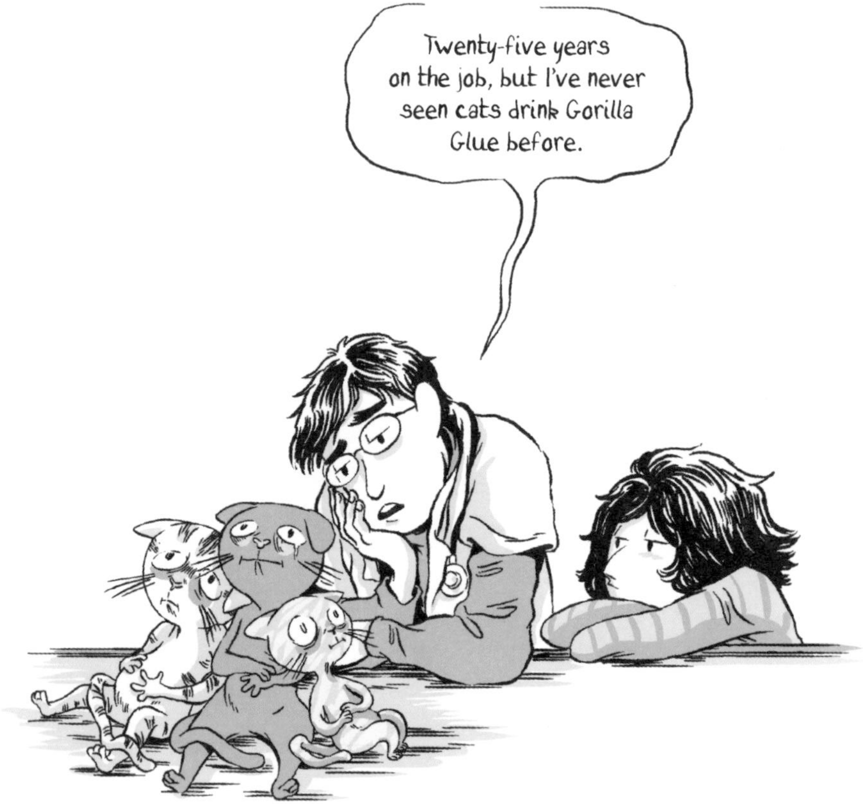
Twenty-five years on the job, but I've never seen cats drink Gorilla Glue before.

Madame lazes

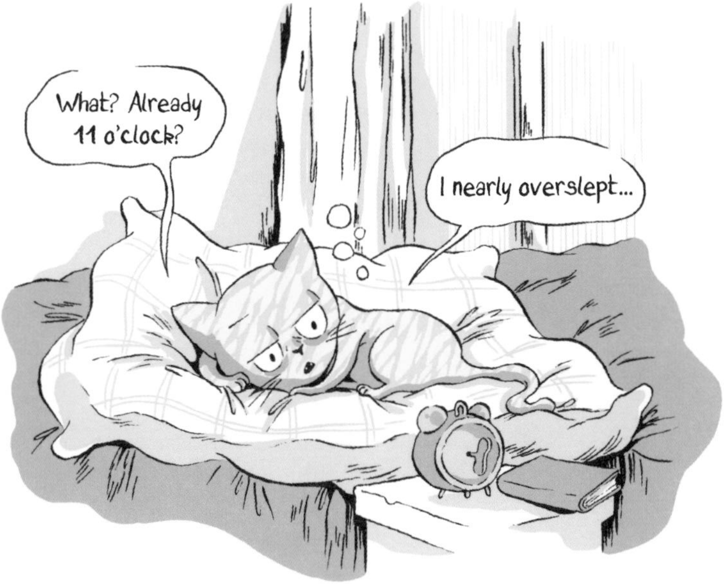
What? Already 11 o'clock?
I nearly overslept...

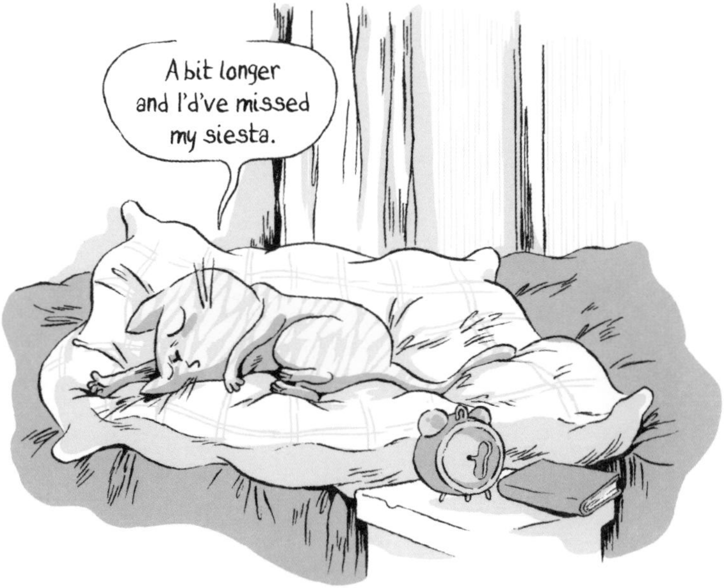
A bit longer and I'd've missed my siesta.

Madame watches

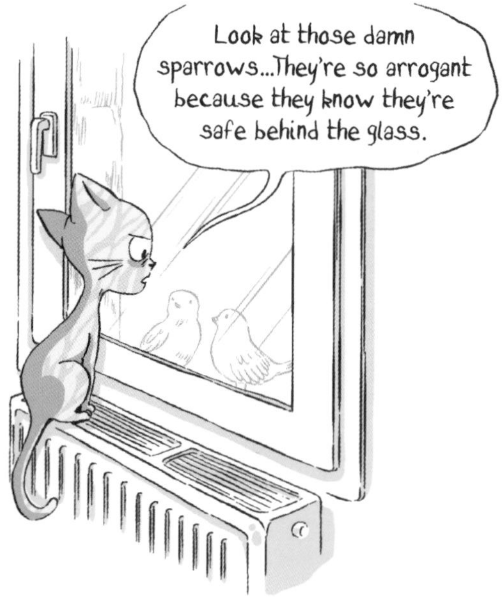
Look at those damn sparrows...They're so arrogant because they know they're safe behind the glass.

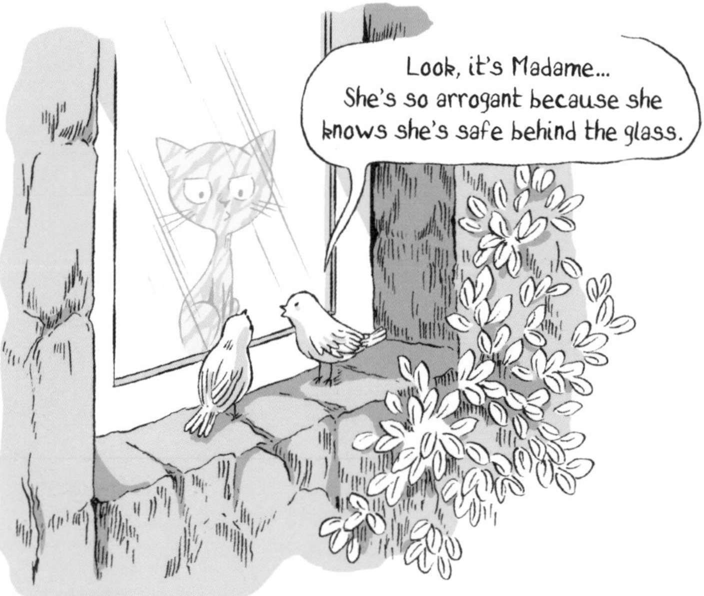
Look, it's Madame... She's so arrogant because she knows she's safe behind the glass.

Madame scuppers

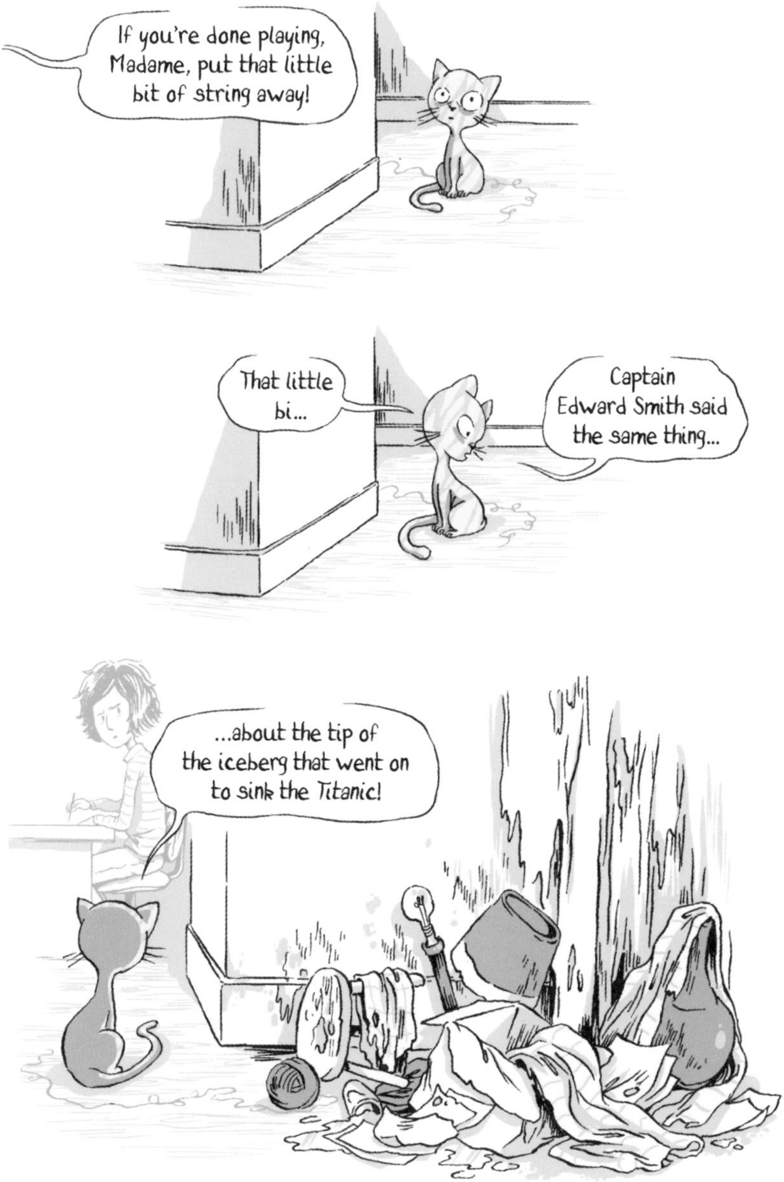
If you're done playing, Madame, put that little bit of string away!
That little bi...
Captain Edward Smith said the same thing...
...about the tip of the iceberg that went on to sink the Titanic!

Madame celebrates

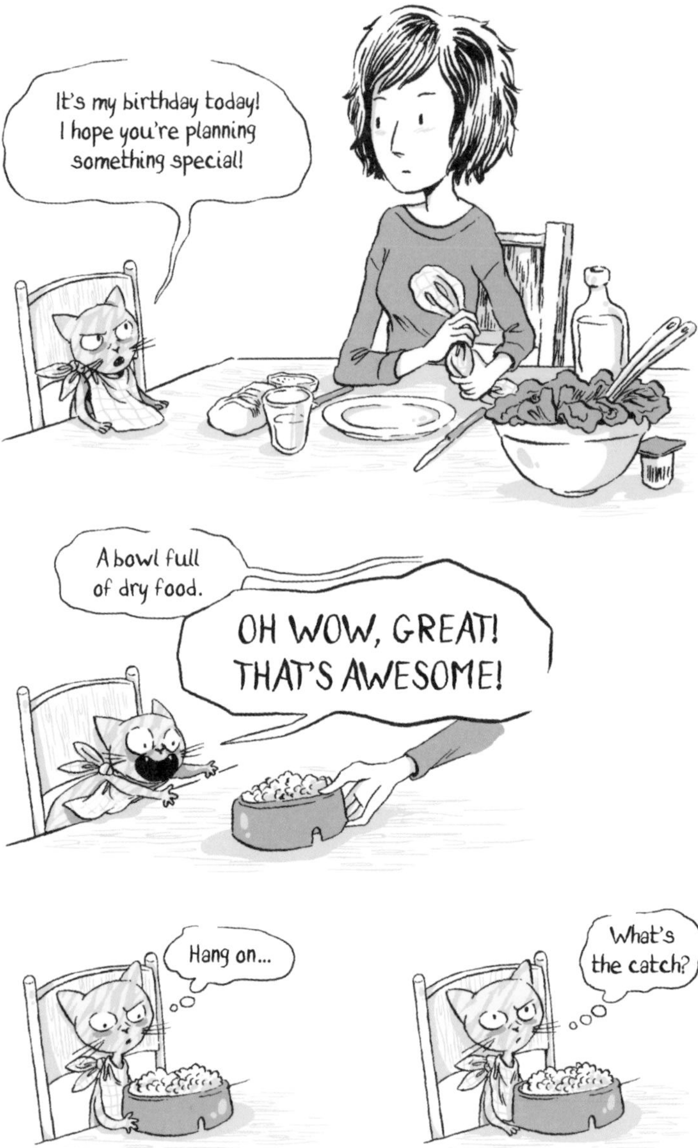
It's my birthday today! I hope you're planning something special!
A bowl full of dry food.
OH WOW, GREAT! THAT'S AWESOME!
Hang on...
What's the catch?

Madame scrams

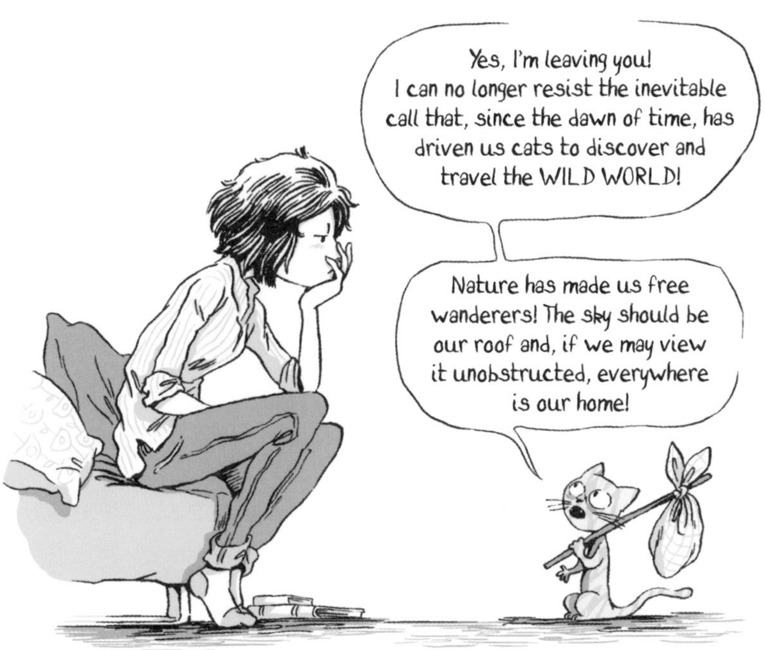
Yes, I'm leaving you! I can no longer resist the inevitable call that, since the dawn of time, has driven us cats to discover and travel the WILD WORLD!
Nature has made us free wanderers! The sky should be our roof and, if we may view it unobstructed, everywhere is our home!

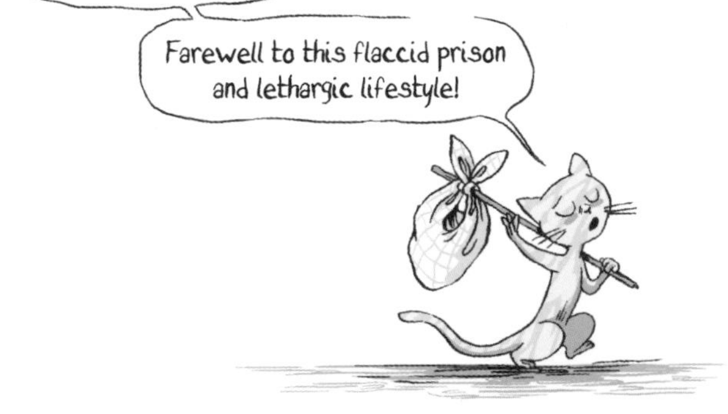
Farewell, artificial human world!
Farewell to this flaccid prison and lethargic lifestyle!

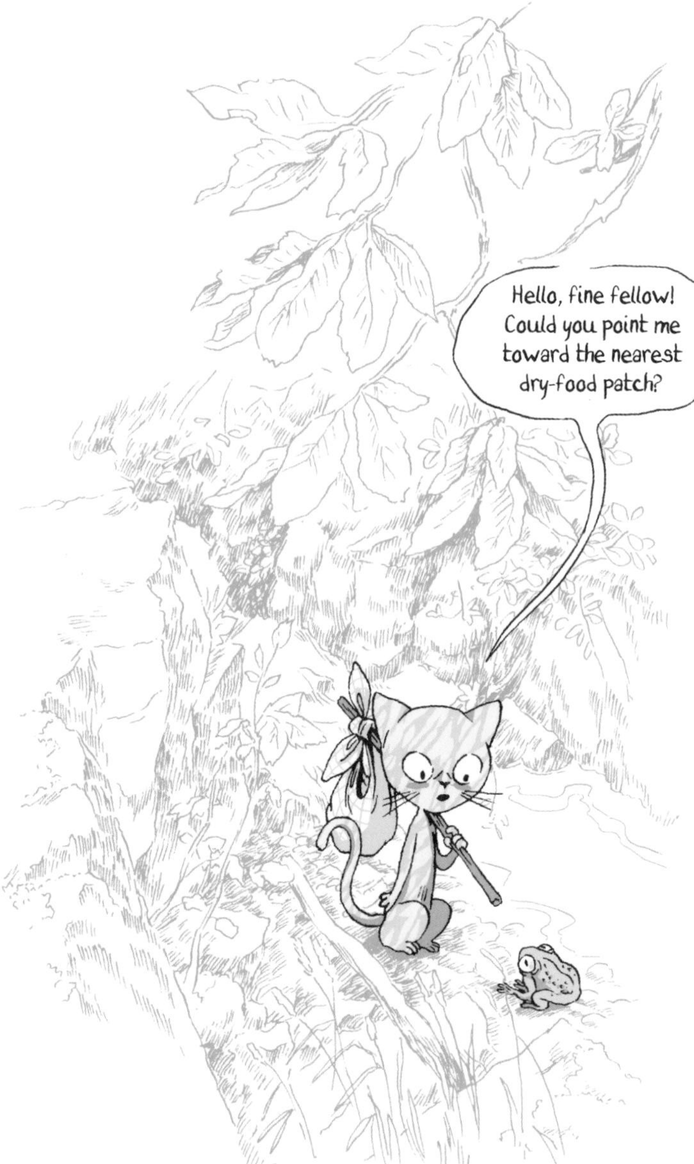
Hello, fine fellow! Could you point me toward the nearest dry-food patch?

Madame relishes

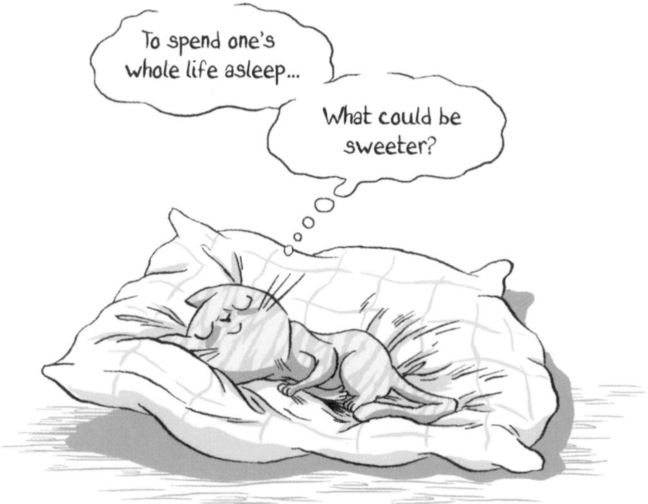
To spend one's whole life asleep...
What could be sweeter?

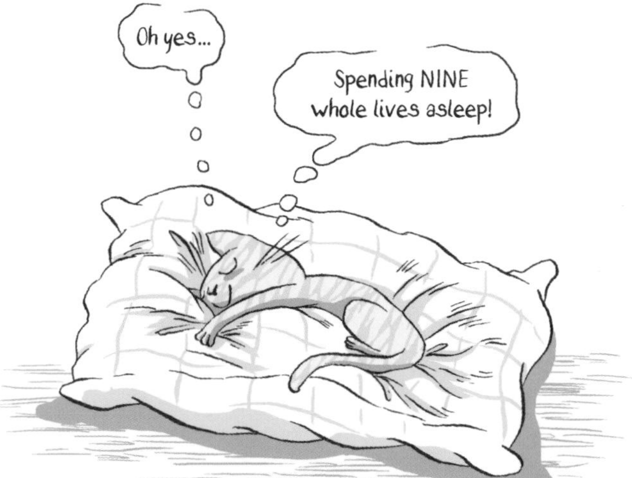
Oh yes...
Spending NINE whole lives asleep!

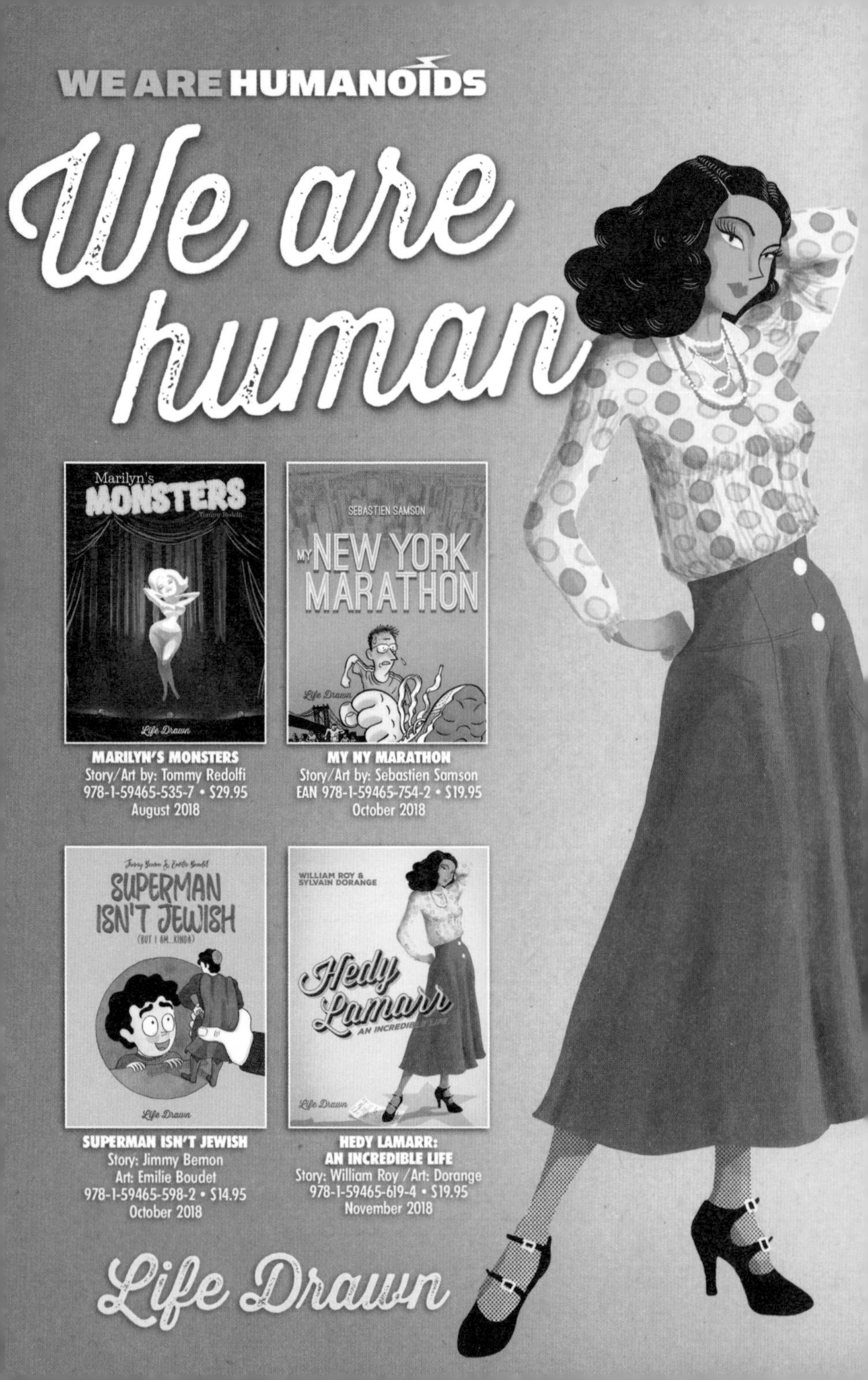
WE ARE HUMANOIDS
We are human
Marilyn's MONSTERS
Tommy Redolfi
Life Drawn
MARILYN'S MONSTERS
Story/Art by: Tommy Redolfi
978-1-59465-535-7 • $29.95
August 2018
SEBASTIEN SAMSON
MY NEW YORK MARATHON
Life Drawn
MY NY MARATHON
Story/Art by: Sebastien Samson
EAN 978-1-59465-754-2 • $19.95
October 2018
SUPERMAN ISN'T JEWISH
(BUT I AM...KINDA)
Life Drawn
SUPERMAN ISN'T JEWISH
Story: Jimmy Bemon
Art: Emilie Boudet
978-1-59465-598-2 • $14.95
October 2018
WILLIAM ROY & SYLVAIN DORANGE
Hedy Lamarr
AN INCREDIBLE LIFE
Life Drawn
HEDY LAMARR: AN INCREDIBLE LIFE
Story: William Roy / Art: Dorange
978-1-59465-619-4 • $19.95
November 2018
Life Drawn